THE ESSENCE
OF MEDITATION

THE ESSENCE OF MEDITATION

Advanced Practices for
New and Experienced Meditators

ANDRES PELENUR

✧

TORONTO

Published by Andres Pelenur

910-2345 Yonge St., Toronto, Ontario M4P 2E5

The content of this book is purely educational in nature. Specifically, this book is not intended to diagnose, cure, treat, or prevent any medical problem or psychological disorder nor is it intended as a substitute for seeking professional health care advice.

Cover design: Kerry Jesberger, Aero Gallerie

Interior design: Williams Writing, Editing & Design

Indexing: Roberts Indexing Services

Bhagawan Nityananda photograph: M.D. Suvarna, Niranjan Suvarna, Foto Corner, Khar(W, Mumbai

Author photograph: Diana Kondor

First published in 2016

Printed in the United States of America

CIPO Registered

ISBN: 978-0-9940571-1-2

To my mother,
who showed me the Guru's lotus feet

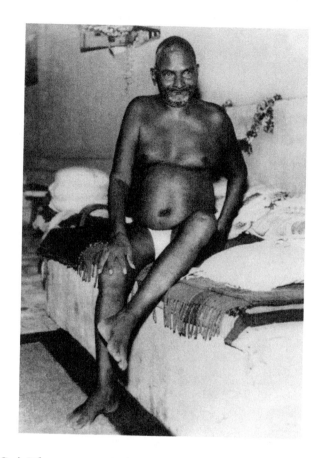

Sri Bhagawan Nityananda of Ganeshpuri

Sarva-pūjyam sadā pūrṇaṁ
Hyakhaṇḍānanda-vigraham,
Sva-prakāshaṁ cid-ānandaṁ
Nityānandaṁ namāmyaham.

An object of worship for all, forever
perfect, an embodiment of bliss, indivisible,
shining by his own light, reveling in blissful
consciousness—to that Nityananda I bow.

CONTENTS

x

THE ESSENCE
OF MEDITATION

NOTE ON THE TRANSLITERATION OF DEVANĀGARĪ SCRIPT

Diacritical marks are employed to indicate long vowel sounds in Sanskrit words in the letters *ā*, *ī*, *ū*. Dots above or below consonants signal stops. The consonant *c* is pronounced *ch*, as in *nirvicāra*. In a few instances, due to established convention, the consonant *c* has been replaced with a *ch*, as in *brahmacharya*. For ease of pronunciation, the sibilants *ś* and *ṣ* have been replaced with *sh*, as in *shaktipāt*.

PREFACE

This book owes its existence to the three golden pillars that support my spiritual life: the endless grace of my Guru Sri Bhagawan Nityananda of Ganeshpuri; Abhinavagupta's Anuttara Trika, otherwise known as the Kashmir Shaivism tradition; and the teachings of Sri Ramana Maharshi (hereafter Sri Ramana). In addition, I owe a debt of gratitude to the quiet yet powerful legacy that Sri Sadhu Om left behind. Sadhu Om was a direct disciple of Sri Ramana whose greatness continues to be discovered in the West, thanks in no small part to the efforts of the brilliant Michael James, also a disciple of Sri Ramana, who lived and studied with Sadhu Om for more than eight years. I also feel indebted to the equally brilliant David Godman for his impeccable scholarship and tireless efforts in making Sri Ramana's teachings available to a wider Western audience.

To be clear, Sadhu Om was no ordinary devotee. In addition to living with Sri Ramana for almost five years, Sadhu Om (like Sri Muruganar and Swami Annamalai) is considered to have attained complete Self-awareness. His greatness lies not only in his attainment of the Self, but on the strength of the indelible spiritual teachings he left behind. In particular, Sadhu Om's book *The Path of Sri Ramana* shines a deeply nuanced light on how to properly understand and practice Sri Ramana's method of Self-enquiry.

The book you are now holding in your hands is not just another presentation of Sri Ramana's teachings. Nor does it devote much time to explaining the philosophy of Kashmir Shaivism, which is so beautifully articulated in a handful of other books.[1] When teachings are discussed, they are strictly in the service of improving our ability to meditate, since what matters ultimately is not how much intellectual knowledge we accumulate but rather how much meditative absorption we experience.

Specifically, this book focuses on several principles and methods of meditation which I have been practicing for over twenty years, drawing upon three primary sources: my own direct experience; the teachings of Swami Lakshmanjoo, an authentic Shaivite Master; and the revelations given by Sri Ramana (including Sadhu Om's clarifications). By synthesizing the essence of both Tantric and Vedantic approaches to meditation, we stand to benefit from an extremely powerful and well-rounded philosophy of meditation that, in my experience, greatly accelerates our ability to become established in Self-awareness.

Although Bhagawan Nityananda's presence and grace support every aspect of my life, readers may notice that throughout the text I devote more time to discussing Sri Ramana and Sadhu Om's teachings, with very little reference to my own Guru. The reason is because Bhagawan Nityananda did not engage in lengthy discourses. His immense power emanated from his presence, and simply standing before him was enough to still the mind. Most of the time people sat around him in silence, absorbing the flow of grace that continually emanated from his divine form. When on occasion he did speak, his words were short, terse, and cryptic. Moreover, many of his sayings, which are published under the title *The Chidākāsh Gīta*, were set down from memory by various devotees and later translated into English, so they cannot be said to constitute a direct record of his speech. While *The Chidākāsh Gīta* is a profound text which reveals many secrets and deserves our careful study, Bhagawan himself was

---

1. Two of my favorites are: *The Doctrine of Vibration*, by Mark S. G. Dyczkowski, and *Trika Saivism of Kashmir*, by Moti Lal Pandit.

completely disinterested in the creation of books or written records of any kind.

In contrast, although Sri Ramana also spent many hours in silence, emitting grace to whomever approached him, over the years an invaluable body of well-articulated questions and answers has been preserved, as well as Sri Ramana's direct writings. The same can be said regarding the price-less revelations given by Swami Lakshmanjoo. So while Sri Bhagawan Nityananda serves as the direct current of grace that enables my meditation to unfold, Sri Ramana and Swami Lakshmanjoo serve as the voices of absolute wisdom. They are all complementary rays of light that emanate from the same Guru principle, which is of course one and indivisible.

INTRODUCTION

If we have been practicing yoga for some time, we will be familiar with the teaching that everything is Consciousness, and that to experience ourselves as Consciousness requires a deep stilling of the mind. Yet no matter how eagerly we embrace this truth, our moment-to-moment experience of being a separate individual persists. Yet, at some point in our spiritual lives, there comes a time when the impulse to move beyond the distant promise of enlightenment and into the actual experience of unity Awareness begins to assert itself with great force. In other words, the question of how to make the attainment of *samādhi* (meditative absorption) a reality becomes our most pressing concern.

Although almost everyone is familiar with the concept of meditation, I have come to realize after speaking to numerous people over the years, that there is much confusion on exactly how to meditate. Should we limit ourselves to passively witnessing our thoughts or should we actively repeat a mantra? If we rely on a mantra, how exactly do we engage with it? Does meditation require phenomenal feats of concentration or is it something that should feel effortless? Should we try to consciously control the Kundalini Shakti (the dynamic power of Consciousness located in the subtle body) or should we simply surrender to it, allowing its grace and wisdom to guide us?[2] Is it best to stick to one method or should we try different things as we go along?

2. The scriptures assert that a human being is composed of four bodies: The physical body, which is experienced in the waking state; the subtle body, which is made up of light and includes the mind and senses and

When I ask people to convey their experiences, most invariably tell me about their struggle to arrest their thoughts, of catching fleeting glimpses of peace, or of seeing the flash of an inner light. But few have shared stories of resting in a deep stillness for prolonged periods of time or of feeling their identity shift into the bliss of formless Awareness, which raises the question: Is the promise of a truly transcendent meditation simply beyond our reach?

The answer is an emphatic "no!" I believe that instead of being reserved for a select few, a great number of aspirants can achieve states of meditative absorption they never thought possible. With this in mind, what I hope to share through these pages is a simple yet highly effective approach to meditation that is as powerful as it is direct. While the practices I recommend are not drawn exclusively from any single yogic tradition, they draw heavily from the teachings of the great twentieth-century sage Sri Ramana Maharshi and his disciples (in particular Sadhu Om), as mentioned in the preface, as well as from the Shaivite Master Swami Lakshmanjoo. By unifying the strengths of both the Tantric and Vedantic traditions, we can easily eliminate blind spots, refine our understanding of the nuances of practice, and establish a rock-solid foundation that will forever support us as we grow in Self-awareness.

The meditation practices presented in this book are available to all and do not require either formal initiation or insider access to any particular yogic lineage in order for them to be effective. All that is required is a proper grasp of technique, a strong desire to meditate, and an unshakable commitment to daily practice. It is my sincere hope that the following pages will enable us to strengthen our contact with

which we occupy during dreaming; the causal body which is a blissful void experienced in deep sleep, and the fourth or transcendental body which is nothing but pure Consciousness and which is experienced by yogins when they achieve a high level of meditative absorption.

the inner Self, allowing us to experience the true promise of
meditation, which is nothing less than complete absorption
into Paramashiva, the supremely blissful and radiant Awareness at the heart of our being.

CHAPTER ONE

A Review of First Principles

Now that yoga studios have proliferated and can be found in almost every neighborhood across the globe, thousands of *āsana* practitioners are beginning to turn their attention toward the true aim behind the physical postures, which is to purify the *nāḍīs* (subtle energy channels) so that the body can tolerate the forces brought about by higher states of consciousness.[3]

When we talk about inner consciousness, we are not referring to the externalized awareness of thoughts, our body, or the world around us, but to the inner awareness of our own deepest being. In other words, awareness, in its pure sense, is the felt presence that we exist, and we naturally carry that awareness with us at all times. (From childhood to old age, we always know that we exist.)

Accordingly, to achieve a higher state of awareness means to focus so intently on our feeling of being that it gradually overshadows our limited body-consciousness, leading to the realization that awareness is what we truly are and that the entire universe is in fact contained within that awareness.

Our deepest awareness, or what I like to refer to as pure Awareness or pure Consciousness, is formless, changeless, and eternal. It exists beyond all notions of time, space, and

---

3. The subtle body, which is made of light, has thousands of energy channels running through it that resemble the physical vascular and nervous systems.

duality, yet it is neither a void or a mere nothingness, but a pulsating fullness of radiant bliss and unfathomable peace that shines forever. In fact, our meditation practice cannot really begin until we accept (or at least open our minds to the possibility) that Awareness is not a product of the brain, but on the contrary, that the brain and the entire universe are products of Awareness (just as the objects in a dream are nothing but an appearance within consciousness).

If, as the sages declare, we have always been nothing but Consciousness, then why do we fail to experience the vast ocean of bliss and peace that are supposed to be integral to its nature?[4] The answer is because our status as pure Awareness has been veiled or obscured by a movement of God's will. Specifically, the power of *māyā* (veiling) along with the ego (the force of self-appropriation which is like a magnet that fuses Awareness to the mind and body) cause the light of Consciousness to experience itself as a finite entity, or as one object among many. The experience of duality and limited identification is called bondage, and our liberation from bondage is simply a severing of our identification with our body and mind, enabling Consciousness to shine again without taint, just as the blue sky shines unobstructed in the absence of clouds.

So how is the severing accomplished? Fully realized sages such as Sri Ramana have taught that to attain liberation does not require a struggle against the manifold aspects or layers of *māyā*.[5] Instead, the only requirement is to neutralize or purify the ego; the latter occurs when our constant flow of thoughts is gradually arrested through proper *sādhanā*

4. See *Taittiriya Upanishad* 3.6.1.
5. *Māyā* is a veiling principle of consciousness that is responsible for the split between subject and object. *Māyā* subjects the individual soul to limitations of action, knowledge, time, attachment, and natural law. From *māyā* also emerge the three defilements, *āṇava*, *māyīya* and *kārma malas* as well as the three gunas or states of *sattva*, *rajas*, and *tamas*.

6

(spiritual practice).[6] Achieving total stillness of mind, or meditative absorption, is known in Sanskrit by various names including *samādhi*, *samāpatti*, or *samāvesha*.

To illustrate how the ego keeps its hold on Consciousness, Sri Ramana likens the ego to a caterpillar which is able to crawl from leaf to leaf so long as it maintains contact with a leaf. The moment both leaves (i.e., thoughts) are removed, the caterpillar falls to the ground.[7] Likewise, when all thought is arrested, the ego has nothing to hold onto, and all of a sudden we are able to move from limited body awareness into the experience of pure Consciousness.

If cessation of thought is the key to neutralizing the ego, what is the most efficacious way to achieve it? The answer is somewhat elusive since effective spiritual practice does not depend on any single factor, but is rather a combination of proper technique, inner feeling, commitment to practice, devotion to God, and other variables. And yet, among the totality of factors that make up spiritual practice, both meditation and devotion (which at the highest levels are one and the same) are the keystones that enable us to still the mind. Now while there is no end to what can be written about devotion, for our purposes we will focus our lens on the formal practice of meditation as the principal means of attaining Self-awareness.[8]

Our Greatest Obstacle

What is the single greatest obstacle facing a spiritual seeker? Put simply, the inability to accept that our mind, body, and

6. Sri Ramana Maharshi, *Nāṉ Yār?*, trans. Michael James, verses 4, 5, 6, 8.
7. David Godman, ed., *Be As You Are: The Teachings of Sri Ramana Maharshi* (London: Penguin, 1985).
8. This is not to suggest that there is any dichotomy between meditation and devotion. On the contrary, deep meditation flows from devotion and devotion rises as a result of deep meditation.

world are all a product of Consciousness. Because we are surrounded by inanimate objects, and because we cannot feel anything outside the confines of our own body, it is quite natural to assume that consciousness is a product of our brain's neural activity. The latter reinforces the experience that we are only a physical body, and it is this very experience that we need to overcome.

One of the classic arguments put forth by science is that damage to the physical brain induces immediate changes in consciousness or cognitive abilities, proving that consciousness is a by-product of the brain. The yogic response is that as long as consciousness is married to the body, changes in the body affect how consciousness is able to manifest through that particular body. But that does not mean that the innate witnessing Consciousness is truly affected. The example of a radio is useful: when a radio is working properly, the broadcast of its electromagnetic waves are clear, but if the radio becomes damaged, the sounds may become fuzzy or the radio may not work at all. Yet it cannot be said that the electromagnetic waves are themselves damaged or changed in any way. Only the waves filtering through that particular radio appear distorted. In the same way, pure Consciousness is never affected, even though the consciousness expressed through an injured brain may appear compromised. In fact, the damaged brain, body, hospital bed, and entire world are all a reflection, unfolding within the expanse of pure Consciousness, much as the images within a television set unfold within the screen. Similarly, the Self is the "screen" on which the projection of creation unfolds, and no matter what the images portray, the screen remains blissfully unaffected.

Another way to look at it is by comparing the Self to the moon. When reflected onto water, the moon can either appear wavy or motionless, depending on the water's condition, while in reality the moon is neither one nor the other. Similarly, Consciousness may appear affected in any number of ways, but in reality it stands behind creation in its pure state. On this point, Sri Ramana stated that to believe that Consciousness is a product of the brain is like believing that the white movie screen exists within the film image.[9]

Our ability to get past the wrong understanding that our consciousness is a by-product of our brain is essential if our meditation is to flourish. The study of high-level texts such as the *Shiva Sūtras*, the *Pratyabhijñāhṛdayaṃ*, the *Yoga Sūtra*, or the collected sayings and writings of Sri Ramana are of enormous assistance in helping us understand the true nature of existence. At a minimum, we must be able to entertain the possibility that the clear division between conscious subjects and insentient objects is not as it appears to be. As our mind grows one-pointed, i.e., concentrated, through sustained practice, we will inevitably begin to experience that everything is a manifestation of Consciousness and that all objectivity is actually contained within an unlimited and eternal subjectivity.

Even after we accept that the universe is an expression of Consciousness, a second and more serious obstacle emerges, namely the feeling that we are a small self in search of a higher Self. When we read about the bliss, peace, and perfection of pure Consciousness, the chasm between the descriptions of pure Awareness and our ordinary, limited sense of being is so vast that we cannot accept that our moment-to-moment subjective awareness is in fact the same great Self we are searching for. Since our everyday I-feeling is confined to the body-mind and rotates endlessly between the waking, dream, and deep sleep states, we are unable to equate it with the stable, infinite Awareness we are trying to become.

As we shall see, while at present our I-feeling is indeed a veiled and limited expression of pure Awareness, it also

9. Sri Ramana Maharshi, *Ēkāṇma Pañcakam*, trans. Michael James and Sadhu Om, verse 3.

happens to be the doorway into the Self. Specifically, if we focus all our attention onto our I-feeling as if it *already were* the pure Consciousness we are seeking, our I-consciousness will eventually open and reveal the actual Self. Subconscious resistance against this simple realization is one of the toughest challenges we face, so as we practice we must continually guard against the misunderstanding that we are a small self that is one day going to stumble onto a higher Self.

A Word of Caution Regarding Scriptural Traditions

India is a holy land not only because of the vast number of enlightened beings born to its shores, but because of the unparalleled number of sacred texts the country has produced. From the numerous yogic traditions that have flourished in India, two in particular have caught the attention of Western seekers: Advaita Vedanta and, more recently, Anuttara Trika.

While both of these traditions are extremely rich and nuanced, we need to be aware of how easy it is to be drawn into them to the point that studying scriptures becomes our only form of practice. It is as if the scriptures act as a hidden maze whose walls are composed of glittering jewels. We are so seduced by the beauty of the stones that we fail to realize that we are slowly being drawn into a never-ending labyrinth that will prove hard to emerge from. The scriptures fill us with so much awe and give us so much comfort that we remain content to bask in their glory, all the while failing to appreciate that the scriptures can never grant us the Self-awareness we are striving for. *The scriptures are dead*, proclaims a famous old saying. Sri Ramana made the same point when responding to a seeker who complained that after much scriptural study, no Self-knowledge had arisen. He stated:

> *Ātmā jñāna* (Self-knowledge) will come to you only if it is there in the *śāstras* (scriptures). If you see the *śāstras*,

śāstra jñāna (knowledge of the scriptures) will come. If
you see the Self, Self-knowledge will shine.[10]

In other words, the only fruit we will receive from studying
the scriptures is scriptural knowledge, while attending to the
Self results in Self-knowledge. It is a point worth remembering, especially given the Western mind's tendency to value
intellectual knowledge above all else. If, for example, we
spend our lives mesmerized by the exact constitution of
the 36 *tattvas* (principles of consciousness), or by trying to
master the entire *Tantrāloka* (Abhinavagupta's magnus opus),
we may learn much and experience a great deal of joy and
satisfaction, but in the end we will grow old and die with the
same degree of limited body-mind identification as when we
first stumbled upon the scriptures.

Although great pundits dot the banks of India's holy rivers
and roam the halls of prestigious universities, have they, in
the end, attained anything more than a vast storehouse of
intellectual knowledge? The contributions of yogic scholars
are great, no doubt, and we should honor them with the
enormous respect they deserve; but we should never lose
sight of the fact that mere study will not effect a change in
our consciousness. On this point, Sri Ramana stated:

> Just as one who needs to sweep up and throw away rub-
> bish [would derive] no benefit by analyzing it, so one
> who needs to know oneself [will derive] no benefit by
> calculating that the *tattvas*, which are concealing oneself,
> are this many, and analyzing their qualities, instead of
> collectively rejecting all of them. It is necessary to con-
> sider the world [which is believed to be an expansion or
> manifestation of such *tattvas*] like a dream.[11]

10. Sri Ramana quoted in David Godman, *Living by the Words of Bhagavan*
(Palakottu: Sri Annamalai Swami Ashram Trust, 1995).
11. Sri Ramana, *Nāṉ Yār?*, trans. Michael James, verse 17.

This is not to suggest, however, that scriptural study is entirely unnecessary. A solid intellectual foundation is essential to be able to meditate deeply. If we do not understand basic principles, or if we do not know how to manage the various phenomena that arise during meditation, we will not be able to make much progress. Moreover, the scriptures allow us to enter into a world rich in meaning and revelation. Many of our burning questions about God, creation, and the soul are finally answered; but questions inevitably lead to more questions, and before we know it we are drawn even more deeply into the scriptures. Accordingly, the caution here is that while we should certainly study the traditions we are attracted to, we must never forget that the only way to make real, tangible progress in our *sādhanā* is to fiercely devote ourselves to our meditation practice.

After all, the primary purpose of tradition is to provide a metaphysical framework that allows us to orient our practice, but if the theory is not actionable, it is of little use. All philosophical systems present models of reality that of course do not capture Reality as it is. The difference is akin to studying the map of Paris in great detail as opposed to taking an actual stroll in Paris. Knowing this, we should understand that no matter how correct or precise our tradition is, mental concepts will never come close to capturing pure Awareness in its actual state. For this reason there is no purpose in arguing, for example, whether Vedanta's assertion that Brahman is entirely passive and that *māyā* is an inexplicable illusion is correct or whether Shaivism's opposing view that *māyā* is a direct expression of the Lord's *svātantrya* Shakti, or power of freedom, is a better understanding of the truth.

We can spend a lifetime arguing these points, but to what end? All we will attain is pride of learning and an intellectual certainty that contributes little to our actual experience of Self-awareness. In fact, we can grow so proud of our tradition that we start to belittle other paths. Instead, why not learn from the example of great beings? Swami Lakshmanjoo comes to mind: for even though he was the foremost living master of Kashmir Shaivism, he took pains to travel almost 2000 miles to Tiruvannamalai to sit at the feet of Sri Ramana (whose teachings mostly follow Vedantic tenets). He later said: "I felt those golden days were indeed divine."[12]

In the end, the metaphysical nuances of our traditions are only of secondary importance, and the proof lies in the ample evidence of fully realized yogins who hail from seemingly opposing traditions (Buddhism and Shaivism are prime examples). In truth, a time will come when we will have to transcend all concepts and assertions. What matters instead is how much energy we put into our practice; so long as our philosophical framework gives us the comfort and confidence to sit quietly and point our mind inward, then our chosen path has fulfilled its foundational purpose.

Further Observations Regarding Vedanta and Kashmir Shaivism

Whether we align ourselves with Kashmir Shaivism or Vedanta carries important implications for our meditation practice. Kashmir Shaivism favors an inclusive view, whereby nothing is outright rejected as an obstacle to attaining Self-awareness. Advanced yogins are supposed to be able to use all cognitions and experiences as access points into pure Awareness. When the mind has become sufficiently one-pointed, the yogin acquires the ability to penetrate the center of any experience, gaining access to the pure Consciousness that is its substrate. For example, instead of being carried away by a sudden rush of anger (which normally reinforces our sense of being a separate individual), the yogin isolates the very first stirrings of anger, experiencing it as a vibration of energy that leads

12. Betina Baumer and Sarla Kumar, eds., *Samvidullasah: Manifestation of Divine Consciousness: Swami Lakshmanjoo, Saint-Scholar of Kashmir Saivism: A Centenary Tribute* (New Delhi: D.K. Printworld, 2011).

directly into pure Awareness. Likewise, if the yogin brings intense awareness into the very initial stirrings of lust, joy, sorrow, or any other emotion, he will be able to plunge into Self-awareness.

In theory, all cognitions, feelings, and activities can be used by a yogin in a likewise manner to gain access to Consciousness. The *Vijñāna Bhairava* is a classic Tantric scripture that sets out 112 centering techniques to access the Self. Everything from the breath, thoughts, emotions, visualizations, to physical sensations and sensory inputs can be harnessed as possible access points into pure Consciousness. Entry is gained through various methods that include penetrating the juncture between two points or objects (such as the space between two thoughts or between the ingoing and outgoing breaths) or entering into the void by a sudden act of awareness (such as staring at an expanse of blue sky).[13] In other words, by digesting all cognitions into Consciousness, the Tantric yogin is supposed to be able to rise above the need to renounce anything and can in fact leverage all the joys and pains of the world as launching pads into pure Awareness.

Such an all-embracing attitude, which lies at the heart of tantra, is on the one hand very attractive while, on the other, also prone to serious drawbacks. The teaching that there is no need for a seeker to shun the senses, but simply shift into the understanding that everything is Shiva (pure Consciousness), is theoretically correct but extremely difficult to apply in practice. This is because the required shift is not an intellectual one but one of an existential nature which can only come about after a prolonged and sustained meditation practice. Otherwise, we will only be pretending that everything before us is Shiva while giving ourselves free license to indulge our

13. Swami Lakshmanjoo, *Vijñāna Bhairava: The Practice of Centering Awareness*, trans. Bettina Baumer (Varanasi: Indica Books, 2002). See as examples *dhāraṇās* 61, 62, and 84.

senses in the name of attaining spiritual awareness. If we do this, we will only be deceiving ourselves.

It is important to understand that if we practice the *dhāraṇās* (contemplations) offered in the *Vijñāna Bhairava*, we will most likely be unable to achieve the desired result because the *Vijñāna Bhairava* is not meant for neophyte yogins, but for highly advanced meditators who are practicing to stabilize their opened-eyed *samādhi*, having already mastered closed-eyed *samādhi*.[14] In other words, the *Vijñāna Bhairava* is a manual for yogins who stand at the very edge of enlightenment.

Simply repeating to ourselves that "everything is Shiva" or that "I am Shiva" will not bring about any results, except for a little purification of consciousness. Such thoughts are only transformative if they are invested with the power of Awareness, which manifests only after we have been able to successfully make contact with the Self. And the latter only comes about after diving deeply into the practice of meditation.

In this light, one of the pitfalls of the surging popularity of Kashmir Shaivism is the false sense of security that the all-embracing philosophy might create. Shaivism is not a shortcut to the steady exertion of right effort required of a yogin. The *Shiva Sūtras* proclaim *prayatnaḥ sādhakaḥ*, meaning: sustained effort brings about attainment in God Consciousness.[15] In truth, we will never experience everything as our own Self until we are first able to utterly still our mind, and stilling our mind entails an initial turning *away* from the senses. To teach aspirants that they should begin by seeing everything as Shiva, when they have no actual experience of pure Consciousness, is akin to telling an aspiring physician

14. The concept of open-eyed *samādhi* versus closed-eyed *samādhi* is fully explained in chapter eight.
15. *Shiva Sūtras* 2:2.

to start practicing medicine without first secluding himself in medical school. Even worse is to teach people that they can regain their Shiva consciousness through contact with the senses. Instead, it is much wiser to turn within and focus on our innate Awareness to the exclusion of all external objectivity. Only after tangible contact has been made with our own deeper Awareness can we go about our day practicing the gaze that everything outside is actually within us, or that everything outside is nothing but pure Consciousness.

The Shaivite Masters were themselves fully aware of the proper order of practice. In *The Doctrine of Vibration*, the great scholar Mark Dyczkowski writes, "Kshemaraja stresses that the Doctrine of Vibration teaches that liberation can only be achieved by first withdrawing all sense activity in introverted contemplation (*nimīlanā samādhi*) to then experience the 'Great Expansion' (*mahāvikāsha*) of consciousness while recognizing this to be a spontaneous process within it."[16] In other words, the apprehension that the external world is nothing but one's own supreme consciousness is only established after closed-eyed, introverted meditative absorption is achieved.

Accordingly, any yogin who has experienced the light of Consciousness knows that one's energies have to be gathered and guarded, the senses restrained, and the mind quieted in meditative absorption before the natural bliss and peace of the Self are able to manifest. As with everything, there are proper and improper ways to control the senses and impulses, some being quite harmful and others beneficial, and for this reason a proper understanding of the mechanics of yoga is essential.

Vedanta, for its part, carries its own drawbacks, especially in how the teaching is transmitted during *satsang* (spiritual

16. Mark S. G. Dyczkowski, *The Doctrine of Vibration: An Analysis of the Doctrines and Practices of Kashmir Shaivism* (Albany: State University of New York Press, 1987).

teachings given in a group setting). Unlike Shaivism, Vedanta's methodology can be compared to peeling away the layers of an onion until nothing but pure Consciousness stands revealed. Everything contained within the sphere of objectivity is rejected as not being the Self, from material objects up to our own body, breath, and mind, enabling our true identity as Brahman to shine forth. In this way, Vedanta seeks to separate the Consciousness that has become indistinguishably entwined with creation in the same way that the mythical swan is able to separate water from milk.[17]

In terms of its philosophy, Vedanta views anything that is not pure subjectivity as the product of *avidyā* (nescience). This *māyā*, or spiritual ignorance, is neither entirely real nor unreal. It is an indefinable superimposition on pure Consciousness that can only be removed through a sudden flash of insight. In its practical sense, *māyā* can be reduced to two primary functions: to obscure pure Consciousness and to outwardly emit all the forms of duality. (Michael James uses the analogy of a movie theater: the darkening of the room, which is the veiling of the Self, is necessary to be able to view the screen, and the images projected onto the screen stand for the manifestation of the universe.)[18]

Like a detailed landscape that instantly appears in a dream, there is no point of origin for the appearance of *māyā*; it simply exists without beginning, in the same way that a mountain, which would normally take thousands of years to form, suddenly towers over our dream landscape. And since the only way to escape a dream is by waking up, the only way to

---

17. The *Rigveda* mentions a mythical *haṃsa* or swan that is able to separate *soma* (nectar) from water when both are mixed together, which stands for the ability to separate pure Consciousness from the material creation, or the pure from the impure. Later texts insert milk instead of *soma*.
18. Michael James, *Happiness and the Art of Being: An Introduction to the Philosophy and Practice of the Spiritual Teachings of Bhagavan Sri Ramana*, 4th ed. (Kindle Edition: Michael D. A. James, 2012).

transcend *māyā* is by awakening out of it through the dawn of pure knowledge.

Vedanta is attractive because it is a logical, internally consistent philosophy that is both beautiful and elegant. It is intellectual wordplay at its finest, and we are constantly reminded to seek and separate the eternal from the transient. The following exchange would be common in any Advaita Vedanta *satsang*:

"I can't seem to stop thinking," says the seeker.

"Who is it that wants to stop thinking?" asks the teacher.

"Me," replies the seeker.

"Who is the 'me' who is asking the question? Is it the body or the mind?"

"It is the mind," says the seeker.

"But who is aware of the mind? Find out who is behind the thinker. Trace the feeling of being an individual 'I' back to its source, and you will discover that only pure Consciousness is found," urges the teacher.

Like a beating drum, Vedanta constantly reminds us that we are not the body or the mind, and the teaching method is designed to shock the mind into silence, allowing pure Consciousness to shine forth. That said, the pedagogical device of negating everything to the extreme can only take aspirants so far.

Shunning all spiritual experience as immaterial because the very person having experiences is to be viewed as unreal, or silencing the questioning mind because the mind itself is to be viewed as a false projection does little (beyond the initial burst of intellectual insight) aside from leaving the yogin with nowhere to turn. Even the finest intellectual appreciation of Vedantic maxims will not alter our present state of awareness. Repeating *neti, neti* ("not this, not this"), which is a classic method of tracing the mind back to pure Consciousness, does not directly lead to Self-awareness. We can attend a thousand Vedanta workshops, but we will not exit the room in a higher state of consciousness. We might receive a lot of "food for thought," but how will we cross the chasm of conceptual knowledge into the realm of actual thoughtless Self-awareness?

The only exception to the above is when the teaching flows directly from the lips of a truly realized Master such as Sri Bhagawan Nityananda, Sri Ramana Maharshi, or Sri Nisargadatta Maharaj, to name a few. When the true Guru speaks, the force and power of their awareness—the force of their grace—can shatter the ego and reveal the Self. But unless we are extremely fortunate, the Advaita teachers we are likely to encounter on the yoga circuit are *learned*, as opposed to *realized*, and their words lack the true Guru's transformative power of grace. Such teachers are, to paraphrase Sri Ramana, nothing but "sound machines" repeating concepts they have studied but not experienced.[19] They are, as the saying goes, like wooden ladles that dish out soup without knowing the taste of it.

If negating the independent existence of the body, mind, and personality does not lead to the dissolution of individual identity, there are still a number of powerful practices that enlightened Masters have revealed as proven methods to attain the Self. Sri Ramana, for example, did not stop with the uttering of Vedantic maxims. He taught a clear and power-ful technique that is greatly misunderstood, but when ap-plied properly, can slice through the ego like a knife through butter. (See the section "Working with the Mind" in chapter four for clarification on Sri Ramana's method of *ātmā-vicāra* [Self-enquiry].)

In reality, there are many things we can do in our efforts to transcend our limited individuality. Even within tradi-tions that emphasize total surrender to the Guru or to the Kundalini Shakti, there is still a great deal of technique in-volved. Without skillful means, we can close our eyes and

19. Sri Ramana Maharshi, *Uḷḷadu Nārpadu Anubandham*, trans. Michael James, verse 35.

wait a hundred years, but all we will witness is the darkness behind our eyelids. So while the negation aspect of Vedantic discourse is very helpful, understanding it intellectually is only a first step. There is in fact a practical method to attain the Self which we must put into action as soon as we have established a solid conceptual foundation.

CHAPTER TWO

Is a Living Guru Necessary?

Most people assume that becoming the disciple of a living Guru is an absolute necessity if we truly are to have the chance to become realized. Without question, serving at the lotus feet of an authentic Guru is life's greatest blessing, but there is compelling evidence that a living Guru is not required to attain Self-awareness. This does not mean that the Guru as a power or principle will not be present to guide us, only that a living, in-the-flesh Guru is not necessary. In fact, if a disciple takes his proximity to the Guru for granted, does not understand who the Guru really is, or is living near the Guru for the wrong reasons, he will profit little from the Guru's liberating presence. This is because it is up to the disciple to step into the ever-flowing stream of divine grace through right effort and a heart filled with devotion.

To be clear, by true Guru I mean a yogin who is fully established in Self-awareness. True Gurus have complete control over their *prāna* (life energy), have completely unfolded their Kundalini Shakti, and are anchored in a state of permanent Self-awareness. They have utterly severed their identification to the body and mind, and are established in *sahaja samādhi* (stable, open-eyed, non-dual Awareness). At a minimum, they must have attained *nirvikalpa samādhi* (closed-eyed, thoughtless, non-dual Awareness). Moreover, they possess initiatory power, meaning they can awaken another's Kundalini, impart a living mantra, or transmit a state of absolute knowledge into a mature disciple. According to this definition, advanced yogins who have merely made contact with the Self and possess knowledge of the scriptures cannot be considered Gurus. The same applies to yogins who can awaken Shakti (spiritual energy) but have yet to achieve the highest level of *samādhi*.[20] As long as the breath has not equalized and merged into the central channel (causing the Kundalini to rush upwards, piercing all the chakras), the yogin, however advanced, is bound by *Māyā* Shakti and remains merely a student on the path.[21]

Although it is true that it takes exceptionally good karma to enjoy even a moment in the presence of a true Guru, Sri Ramakrishna observed that spiritually immature seekers who live with the Guru can cause Him to appear like a lamp post that casts a pool of darkness beneath it, while mature devotees living far away are able to bask in the Guru's light and power.[22] In other words, despite living in the physical presence of the Guru, spiritually immature devotees will be unable to make significant progress, and their contact with the Guru's energy will be wasted, like sand slipping through their fingers.

Gurus themselves often say that living in their physical presence is not required. Certain saints conducted their entire *sādhanā* without ever having a living Guru. Tukaram Maharaj was initiated by Lord Chaitanya in a dream. *Dīkshā* (initiation) through dream is an accepted mode of transmission. By initiation I mean *shaktipāt* (the descent of divine grace), where the Guru destroys the disciple's root impurity (the *ānava mala*, according to Shaivism), awakens the "dormant" Kundalini Shakti, and enters the disciple's consciousness. In Vedanta, although *shaktipāt* is not openly discussed, the

20. The ability to awaken Shakti arrives long before the ego has been eviscerated in *samādhi*.

21. The equalization of the breath, its entry into the central energy channel that runs along the spine, and the ascent of the Kundalini Shakti are fully explained in chapter seven.

22. Sri Ramakrishna, *Sayings of Sri Ramakrishna* (Chennai: Sri Ramakrishna Math, 2008).

process is the same, with only its effects being stressed, such as the sudden glimpse of unity Awareness that flashes in the presence of the Guru.

Other saints were only able to spend a short amount of time with their Gurus, including Sri Nisargadatta Maharaj and Sadhu Om, but that did not stop them from attaining everything. Another realized being, Sri Annamalai Swami, was told by Sri Ramana to stop coming for *darshan* (beholding a holy being) at the ashram and to continue his meditation at home. Sri Annamalai's final Self-realization came only after he had moved away from the ashram.[23] Other Gurus initiated disciples and sent them to live far away, as in the case of Swami Janananda of Kanhangad who was asked by Sri Bhagawan Nityananda to leave Ganeshpuri and return to Kerala, some 800 miles away. Some yogins were devoted to Gurus who had passed away even before they were born, yet they still attained full Self-realization. Clearly then, although having a living Guru is the greatest blessing, lack of physical presence is no obstacle in God's ability to guide those who are lovingly striving toward Self-awareness.

In fact, Sri Ramana confirmed that mental contact or association with a realized being is as good as basking in their physical presence. Since the Guru is not the physical body, the same opportunity to make contact and enter into the Guru's stream of grace remains even after the death of the body.[24]

If the Guru is in actuality our own inner Self, the question arises as to why the need for an external Guru at all? Put simply, why can't our inner Self serve directly as our guide? The answer lies in the fact that the physical Guru, being a reflection of our inner Self, only manifests after we have reached a certain level of spiritual maturity. In other words,

---

23. David Godman, *Living by the Words of Bhagavan* (Palakottu: Sri Annamalai Swami Ashram Trust, 1995).

24. Sri Sadhu Om, *Sri Ramanopadesa Noonmalai* (Tiruvannamalai: Sri Ramana Kshetra, Kanvashrama Trust, 2008).

the physical appearance of a true Guru is a response to an already mature inner state. When water, for example, accumulates enough heat, it naturally breaks into a boil. Likewise, when our longing to experience our own deeper awareness grows strong enough, the outer Guru naturally appears. And since our minds are so used to being externalized, it would be very difficult for us to get through all the trials and tribulations of spiritual life without having an external point of reference to inspire, guide, and empower us along the way. Moreover, the presence of a fully realized Guru proves that our efforts to transcend the mind are not based on scriptural abstractions but on a concrete, achievable reality. In other words, the physical Guru proves to us that enlightenment is real.

For a true devotee whose heart overflows with devotion, initiation can occur at any time and in any place. It goes without saying that real *bhakti* or devotion is not a feeling that can be manufactured. It unfolds naturally in a devotee who has reached a certain degree of spiritual maturity through their efforts in *sādhanā*, either in this or in previous lifetimes. In this way, genuine devotion to an outer Guru is always a reflection of a pre-existing devotion to our own inner Self. Surrendering to a Guru is not a forced emotion. As many seekers can attest, the connection to the Guru is divine, secret, and in many occasions completely unexpected. We meet the Guru or see a picture of the Guru and something shatters our heart. We just know.

It is vital, therefore, to be able to understand who and what the Guru really is. And while the subject of the Guru can fill volumes, I will try to limit myself to a few key observations.

The Nature of the Guru

To begin, the *Shiva Sūtras* proclaim: *Gururupāyaḥ*, the Guru is the means (to liberation).[25] Kshemaraja, in his commentary

---

25. *Shiva Sūtras* 2:6.

on the sutra, states: *Gururvā pārameshvari anugrahikā śaktihi*, meaning: the Guru is the grace-bestowing power of God.

But what exactly does this mean?

Out of God's five powers (creation, maintenance, dissolution, concealment, and grace), the *Guru Tattva* or Guru principle operates as the fifth power of grace. Lord Shiva, through the agency of his own Shakti, emits Himself outward as the universe. Later, he absorbs Himself back into oneness. In terms of function, the Guru denotes the power that resolves Consciousness back into itself, healing the tripartite division between the knower (subject), the act of knowing (knowledge), and the known (object).

In a less subtle form, the Guru is the vibration of mantra which the person of the Guru imparts, and in his least subtle form, the Guru is the outer physical body we associate as our Master. At the same time, we should not lose sight of the fact that ultimately the Guru transcends all functions and forms, since from the highest perspective, the Guru is none other than pure Awareness.

Given the above, and added to the fact that our own awareness is itself pure Consciousness, we can arrive at the understanding that there is no difference or separation between the Guru and our own inner Self. But the understanding cannot be merely intellectual, and the meditation practices presented in this book are designed to bring us closer to that goal.

Accordingly, there is no need to feel anxious about not having a living Guru in our lives. As a matter of fact, it may prove to be a benefit, given the number of false gurus out there. If we are able to meditate effectively, in time a true Guru will manifest before us, either in the form of a living Guru or through a dream or vision (or we may be drawn into a relationship with a Guru who is no longer alive but whose power is still overtly manifested).

Prior to that moment, it is preferable to avoid surrendering to a living Guru until we have had a chance to meditate deeply and make contact with the Self. Otherwise, our ability to detect the so-called guru's level of attainment will be underdeveloped, and we risk being deceived by a pretender. Instead, we should meditate daily with the conviction that the force of our practice will one day move the Lord to manifest a Guru in our lives, whether alive or departed.

In my own case, after coming across pictures of Bhagawan Nityananda of Ganeshpuri, I developed a strong current of devotion to him. I began meditating every day with the mantra *Om Namaḥ Shivāya* that I received from Gurumayi Chidvilasananda at her ashram near South Fallsburg, New York, and after a few months of daily practice, I had a profound and life-changing experience one afternoon after I came home from college (I was twenty years old at the time). Without going into all the details, Bhagawan Nityananda appeared to me in a very dramatic way (I was not meditating at the time). He touched my head with his right hand, and I was thrown into a transcendental state where I became a rushing vibration of pure Consciousness. Though I no longer had a body, my awareness felt as if it were moving at the speed of light, and the movement and intense vibration were accompanied by an extremely loud rushing sound, somewhat akin to the massive roar that can be heard when standing at the base of a waterfall. After what felt like a long time, I returned to bodily awareness, and for a few more seconds I could still feel the tremendous rush of energy moving from the base of my spine all the way up to the crown of my head. I was unable to move a muscle, and only after another few seconds was I released from the flow of energy, regaining movement in my limbs.

My *shaktipāt* initiation from Bhagawan, powerful as it was, did not elevate me into any permanent higher state of Awareness, though it brought me into the direct stream of Bhagawan's liberating grace, moving me from devotee to disciple and opening the door for me to begin my *sādhanā* in earnest. While it is important for yogins to cherish and protect their spiritual experiences, I've chosen to share this one in the hope that it will remove any doubts that initiation can happen at any time, and by the grace of Gurus who are no longer in their physical bodies. Such divine Gurus were never really human in the first place, and the dropping of their physical bodies does nothing to reduce their presence or ability to reach their devotees. In fact, if the seeker's devotion is sufficiently intense, the Guru is drawn almost by force into that disciple's life, which means that, as disciples, we have tremendous power in being able to attract God's grace. In fact, it is said that the Guru has no choice but to bless and protect such disciples, being united to them by the force of their remembrance and devotion.

The lesson, therefore, is to never feel limited by the absence of a living Guru. The Lord is omniscient and omnipotent, and he can raise a yogin in the blink of an eye. The Guru can make Himself known through a vision, a dream, in meditation, or by orchestrating events so that one finds oneself unexpectedly traveling to a far-off place to sit at the feet of a sage.

As stated above, the Guru must be fully realized for us to truly benefit from a relationship with a living Guru. And as we all know, the world is rife with false gurus, claiming not only to have attained the highest state but to be able to give *shaktipāt* in exchange for a fee. On the Vedanta side, there are a number of people claiming to be *jñānins* who are quite skilled in parroting Advaita Vedanta discourse while possessing no actual Self-awareness. Sri Bhagawan Nityananda anticipated all of this when he said:

In the near future even a milestone shall preach. At least a milestone is truthful. It will show you the right path and tell you how far are you from the goal. But these stones of Kaliyuga will cheat in the name of God. They will sell instant liberation, instant Kundalini awakening, teach pranayama and demand money. All this is nothing but a circus. Every other person will claim to be a Siddha (perfected being). They'll want big ashrams, groups of devotees, etc. What is the test then for finding a true Guru? Demand from him whether he can show you God in His true form. Only if he has true renunciation can he be your Guru. When you spit your saliva after eating a betel leaf, you do not take it back into your mouth. So also, when a sadhu gives up anything, he never ever goes hankering after it again. He can give up all his possessions without giving it a thought and walk out. He is ever free and nothing can bind him. The Guru owns everything but possesses nothing. The Sadguru is one who is free from any temptation, free from any involvement, remains completely aloof and is a manifestation of renunciation and detachment. He owns everything in this universe and is his own Master, yet he possesses nothing and is ever free. He is Jagadguru. He is Shiva. The Sadguru is in your heart.[26]

It is best to avoid surrendering to anyone except a true Guru, and once we become a disciple, it is imperative that we look upon that Guru as an embodiment of pure Consciousness. If we are incapable of seeing the Guru as pure Consciousness, confusing the Guru's body with that of an ordinary person, our progress will be severely limited, for we will be equally incapable of seeing the world or ourselves as pure Consciousness.

If we happen to develop a natural devotion toward a Guru who is no longer alive, we should not create a false obstacle by believing that we are doomed to receive less from Him

26. This quote is slightly edited for ease of reading. Adapted from: Dr. Gopalkrishna R. Shenoy, *The Eternal One* (online: http://babanityananda.hpage.com/ Chapter 5).

or Her than their direct devotees did. Initiation through the will of a Guru is termed *saṅkalpa dīkṣā*, and it is no less efficacious than the initiation received by a Guru who is standing in front of you.

Since it may take some time before a true Guru appears in our lives, it is perfectly fine to turn to others who can serve as teachers and mentors, as long as these people (even ones with a fair degree of attainment) openly acknowledge that they are still yogins on the path and that they are not fully realized. Mentors and teachers can offer much in terms of helpful guidance, but they themselves should be an example of humility, surrender, and devotion to their own Gurus.

How can we evaluate our teachers? Above all, we should sense purity and sincerity in their intentions. They can teach us to meditate, to chant, or to better understand the scrip-tures, but they should never advertise themselves as liberated beings. If they do, it will be up to us to decide if they are self-deluded, willfully deceiving others, or if they are in fact realized (possible but very unlikely). We accept people who make such claims at our own peril. In most circumstances, it is better to define the relationship as between fellow as-pirants, or at most between teacher and student, but never between guru and disciple. If we yearn for discipleship, we can focus our devotions toward a Guru who has historically been accepted as authentic (Shirdi Sai Baba, Sri Bhagawan Nityananda, Sri Ramana Maharshi, Sri Neem Karoli Baba, Sri Anandamayi Ma, Sri Shaligram Swami, Sri Annamalai Swami, Sri Nisargadatta Maharaj, and Sri Ramakrishna are just a few of the saints that are well known in the West). As for living gurus, the earth is never without its share of enlightened beings, although many choose to remain hidden from sight. If it is meant for us, we will one day find ourselves standing face-to-face before such an enlightened being. As the saying goes, when the disciple is ready, the Master appears.

Self-Effort versus Grace

The necessity of having a Guru is closely related to the debate about the value of self-effort versus grace. The scriptures ask, which one is more important for spiritual progress?

Although nothing can be accomplished without God's grace, from a practical point of view it stands to reason that self-effort is more important than grace. And while it is true that interest in spiritual matters cannot even arise without God's grace (making grace supreme), the arrival of such grace cannot be predicted or controlled; therefore we cannot include it as a working element in support of our spiritual progress.

Before we consciously take to spiritual life, grace operates primarily in the form of suffering (I say primarily, not exclusively). Meeting the right friend or coming across the right book can also be signs of grace. In short, anything that pivots our attention inward toward our innate I-consciousness is an aspect of grace.

The fact that life constantly sways between joy and sorrow (which is itself a form of suffering), causes us, over lifetimes, to become weary and disillusioned. We feel like a boat that has been thrashed against the rocks once too often, and we eventually turn our eye toward the bigger questions in life: Who am I? What is the purpose of my life? How can I achieve lasting peace and happiness? Suffering can move us toward virtues such as observing morals, showing kindness and compassion, and feeling gratitude for goodness in our lives, which in turn attract even more grace. These are the first stirrings of spiritual life, which truly begins only after we consciously submit to spiritual practice. From this perspective, grace is already embedded in the fabric of nature through all the forms of suffering we encounter, although in this modality progress is exceedingly slow.

Up to this point we are under the care of what I like to think of as the slow wheel of grace; but once we consciously make efforts toward Self-awareness, then the intensity of grace increases in a dramatic fashion. Pain and suffering are alien to our natural state of well-being. The Self certainly does not experience itself in the form of pain and suffering, so our journey into Self-awareness does not have to be marred by pain and suffering from start to finish. Suffering is a device created by Consciousness to ensure that embodied souls are motivated to seek a higher existence. It is an exit mechanism pure Consciousness imposes on itself to make sure it does not get lost in its own creations. But the sooner a yogin is able to reduce suffering and increase peace and bliss, the better. Once contact with the Self has been established through effective meditation, the impressions of bliss left in the mind instill us with a strong desire to keep meditating until final liberation is attained. In this way, an upward spiral is established which binds us to the path.

A common objection to the superior importance of self-effort is that no matter how hard we try, we cannot make any progress without the Guru's grace. Even if we meditate for hours a day, our minds will remain as restless as a boiling pot of water without the blessings of the Guru. Although the latter is true, since the Guru is none other than our own inner Self, it is also important to understand that as long as sincere efforts are made, the Guru's grace is bound to manifest.

Using the analogy of a sailboat, the sailor's only job is to get the boat in the water, raise the mast, and unfurl the sails. And although the wind cannot be forced or coerced, in time it will fill the sails, propelling the boat forward. In the same way, as long as we are engaged in skillful self-effort (I empha-size right effort because even the best seeds, if scattered over parched land, will fail to sprout), the Guru's grace is bound to manifest. As Sri Ramana said: "The internal Guru pulls him in and the external Guru pushes him into the Self. This is the grace of the Guru."[27]

27. Godman, *Be As You Are*.

In this light, the Guru's function in taking on a body is not only to dispense his grace, but to teach yogic practices and principles that will attract even more grace. To paraphrase a well-known teaching, the Guru does not walk the path for us, but only points the way, leaving it up to us to strive toward Self-realization. The aphorism from the *Shiva Sūtras* (quoted earlier) also bears repeating: *prayatnaḥ sādhakaḥ* (sustained effort brings about attainment in God Consciousness), which confirms that conscious effort cannot be avoided.[28]

With this understanding, there is no need to try to force the transformation of our consciousness. Once we learn how to meditate properly, we can relax into our practice, keeping our focus on our daily commitment, with the knowledge that everything else is in the Guru's compassionate hands. On this point Sri Ramana stated that perseverance is the only true sign of progress.[29] That is, the very desire to continue to meditate is a clear sign that we have already stepped into the current of grace.

One of the benefits of this teaching is that it fosters authentic humility. It also helps us avoid the feeling that we are in a constant battle against an enemy who is infinitely stronger than we are (our extroverted, restless mind). In time, we achieve a perfect balance between effort and grace, knowing that the Guru's grace united with our self-effort is like the wings on a bird that lift us beyond the veiling power of *māyā*.

As an aside, from a higher perspective it is also fair to assert that self-effort does not really exist. Since the Lord is aware of the past, present, and future, God already knows exactly what choices we are going to make, which dilutes the idea that we are free to choose at all. From an even higher perspective, since a unified expanse of pure Consciousness is all that exists, the very idea that we are separate individuals

28. *Shiva Sūtras* 2:2.
29. James, *Happiness and the Art of Being*.

with separate wills is itself a fallacy. There can be no "freedom" from God's will, so to speak, if God's will is all that exists. This is why Sri Ramana made it clear that free will is a relative concept because admitting to it also necessitates admitting to the existence of a separate individual.[30] That said, as long as we remain erroneously identified as the body-mind, from a practical perspective, it is very important to understand that self-effort is absolutely necessary.

Self-Awareness: Now or a Hundred Lifetimes from Now?

Buddhist traditions are well known for teaching that Lord Buddha's attainment was so rare and elevated that it would take us ordinary *sādhakas* (aspirants) aeons to achieve his state. There is a well-known parable of a bird who flies over a mountain: once every thousand years, a bird with a long silk scarf hanging from its beak flies over a tall mountain, gently brushing the scarf across the mountain's top. The time it would take the bird to reduce the mountain to a scattering of rocks is the time we can expect it to take for us to complete our spiritual journey.

Needless to say, the story is quite disheartening. It causes us to feel that liberation is never going to happen, or that however hard we try, we are destined to remain stuck near the start of our journey. Even if the moral of the parable is to teach patience and humility and to discourage the spiritual ego, it overreaches. In fact, it is a serious obstacle to believe that Self-awareness is so far away or so unattainable that we have no hope of success. Even our Buddhist cousins are aware of this problem, and worrying about failure or lack of progress on the spiritual path is considered an obstacle

30. Godman, *Be As You Are.*

to the attainment of tranquil abiding.[31] Yet everywhere one turns within Buddhist teaching, there is great emphasis on how long and arduous the path will be (to be fair, the same discourse is sometimes found in Hindu scripture), which ends up being counterproductive.

Instead, we should adopt the opposite attitude of what the Buddhist parable teaches. It would serve us better to believe, from the depths of our heart, that Self-realization is just around the corner and that we can attain it in this very lifetime (perhaps not today or tomorrow, but certainly in this lifetime). Otherwise, we are certain to remain stuck in the non-existent past or future, while ignoring the actual doorway into Self-awareness—which, of course, is located in the present moment.

The feeling that Self-realization is within our grasp is essential if we are to sustain a daily meditation practice. We must get up in the morning brimming with enthusiasm, eager to plunge our mind into its deeper Self. Of course, there will be so-called good days and not-so-good days, where we cannot help but judge the quality of our meditation (getting rid of the judging mind is part of the practice, but it is easier said than done). Since not every session will be to our liking, we can develop a counter-strategy that will allow us to remain deeply engaged with our practice. That strategy is made up of three important insights: first, the Guru's grace is ever with us; second, time is precious and should not be wasted (i.e., death can touch us at any time); and third, Self-realization is absolutely possible in this very lifetime. The *Bhagavad Gītā* states that no effort in yoga goes to waste and that progress in yoga will quickly resume in the next lifetime if the yogin happens to die before attaining liberation.[32]

---

31. Geshe Kelsang Gyatso, *Clear Light of Bliss: The Practice of Mahamudrā in Vajrayana Buddhism* (Glen Spey, NY: Tharpa Publications, 1992).
32. *Bhagavad Gītā*, 2:40 and 6:41–45.

We should approach our meditation seat with the conviction that our session will carry us deeply into the bliss of the Self. Then we will find ourselves filled with enthusiasm, and this feeling in turn will lift our *sādhanā* to greater and greater heights.

CHAPTER THREE

I-consciousness Is Behind Everything

Now that we have reviewed a few foundational concepts, it is time to turn our attention directly toward our ground of experience and ultimate target of yogic practice: our felt sense of being, also referred to as our I-ness, I-feeling, I-sense, or I-consciousness.

If we scrutinize our moment-to-moment existence, we will quickly discover that our own sense of being is something we continuously take for granted. The first lesson of spiritual life is to remember that no matter what is happening, we are always present. Without the awareness of our presence, we cannot even claim to be present, much less to exist. The scriptural term used to define the Self in Sanskrit is *satchidānanda*, which is translated as "being, consciousness, and bliss." *Sat* refers to "I" or "being"; *chit* refers to "Am" or "awareness of being"; and *ānanda*, or "bliss," is how the pure "I Am" experiences itself when it is devoid of all associations. In the Bible, God defines himself as "I am That I am,"[33] and the first aphorism of the *Shiva Sūtras* is *caitanyamātmā*, which means "Supreme Consciousness is the reality of everything."[34]

So in the phrase "I am," the word "I" refers to our pure sense of being, while the word "Am" refers to our consciousness of being. In other words, consciousness has the special quality of being self-aware. And "I am" must always come first:

33. Exodus 3:14 King James Version.
34. *Shiva Sūtras* 1:1.

"*I am* a man" or "*I am* a woman." Only if our sense of being is *present* can it be associated with other qualities or adjuncts—man, woman, happy, sad, tall, short, old, young, healthy, sick, teacher, accountant, engineer, and so forth. Moreover, something that exists and is self-aware cannot require the evidence of another to point out its existence (otherwise by definition it would not be self-aware). If consciousness needed another consciousness to confirm its existence, this would lead to a situation of infinite regress. That is why Sri Ramana states, "To know existence (*sat*), there is no consciousness (*chit*) other than existence itself; existence is therefore consciousness."[35]

Accepting our sense of being as the starting point of everything, Sri Ramana divides all experience into three simple categories: the first, second, and third persons.[36] The first person refers to our sense of being, the "I am" awareness or knowing subject described above. The second person refers to the internal flow of thoughts, concepts, and emotions occurring directly within the mind, and the third person refers to all the objects of perception fed to us through our five senses, including the perception of inhabiting a body. In these three categories, the entirety of existence is captured; it is a very useful way of looking at things that allows us to segregate our I-consciousness from all objects of experience, both material and subtle.

While second and third-person objects are always entering and exiting our field of awareness, we always know for certain that we exist. We never lose sight of our sense of being, even arguably when we faint, are put under general anesthesia, or awake from dreamless sleep. This is because upon waking we immediately detect that there has been a lapse in our everyday, content-filled awareness, which suggests that a consciousness must have been present to report on our blank state of awareness. Otherwise, if awareness had

35. *Upadesa Undhiyar,* verse 23.
36. *Ulladhu Narpadhu,* verse 14.

truly ended the moment before we fainted and resumed the moment we woke up, we would be left with no ability to detect that we were "out." But experience tells us just the opposite: the moment we wake up, we know we existed for a period of time with a non-active mind. And yet, because our sense of self appears to rise and fall as we alternate between wakefulness and sleep, we are left with the strong impression that our consciousness depends on the body and that there is no such thing as a continuous background of Awareness.

Within spiritual literature, the feeling of being the body and mind is what is termed "being unconscious." In contrast, the more we identify with the Awareness behind our thoughts, the more "conscious" we are said to be; to permanently shift our identity from the body-mind into pure Awareness constitutes the primary goal behind all spiritual effort.

I-consciousness in Its Current State Is Known as the Ego

Now that we have identified our I-consciousness as the ground of our existence, we need to understand why it should form the basis of our practice. Let us examine our sense of being more closely. It follows that if we peel back the layers that make up our reality (world, body, breath, and mind), we end up with our I-consciousness, the knowing subject that we feel ourselves to be. This is as far back as we can go.

Since our I-consciousness is supposed to be the same as pure Awareness, why are we not immediately plunged into a state of enlightenment the moment we recognize it? In other words, after drawing our attention to our knowing subject, which only takes a second, why do we remain in exactly the same state as we were before?

The answer lies in the fact that in our present condition, our I-consciousness is completely identified with the body-mind, which is why our I-consciousness is sometimes referred to as the ego itself. That is, while our limited I-consciousness forms the basis of pure Awareness, it also functions as the manifest aspect of the ego. Like a strip of transparent tape pressed onto a glass window, the ego's grip is both strong and difficult to see, which is why shifting attention onto our sense of being for a quick moment is not enough to prevent pure Consciousness from experiencing itself as a limited being.

Yet despite the ego's overwhelming influence, there is a proven method to eliminate it, which is to gradually keep our attention solely on our I-consciousness for extended periods of time until our thought stream naturally dies down. The moment we sink into true meditative absorption, the ego part of the equation dissolves, enabling our I-consciousness to perceive itself in its absolute purity.

So depending on our perspective, it is perfectly correct to refer to our I-consciousness either as the ego or as the seat of pure Awareness.

Shifting Attention Away from Thoughts and onto I-consciousness Is the Fastest Way to Attain Self-Awareness

As stated above, the fastest and most efficient way of getting rid of thoughts is to work directly with our I-feeling; therefore our most pressing concern becomes how to go about this.

Traditionally, the scriptures divide the mind into four aspects: *buddhi* (intellect), *ahaṅkāra* (ego), *manas* (thought stream and perception), and the underlying *chit purusha* (limited consciousness).[37] While this classification is highly useful in helping us to understand and work with the mind, it fails to highlight the one aspect that is instrumental in allowing us to make tangible progress toward Self-awareness: the power of attention.

37. See Swami Lakshmanjoo and John Hughes, ed., *Kashmir Shaivism: The Secret Supreme* (Culver City: Universal Shaiva Fellowship, 2003).

In fact, the power of attention is so important that I prefer to think of it as a separate or fifth aspect of the mind. Technically, the power of attention is no different from the power of knowing, so it belongs to the *chit* aspect of the mind. In other words, the power of attention is consciousness itself, which is what makes it so powerful.

A simple exercise helps illustrate how the power of attention operates:

Sit comfortably with closed eyes. For a moment, focus on your breath and let your mind settle down. Now shift all of your attention onto your left big toe. Notice that while you can still feel yourself as a body, your mind is particularly aware of your left big toe to the exclusion of all other parts. Now shift your attention up to your right ear. See how your mind becomes completely aware of your ear to the exclusion of all other parts. Gently open your eyes.

With this very simple exercise we can see how the mind is able not only to shift its focus in a dramatic way, but to zero in on a target and exclude all other objects of perception. This ability, which even a child possesses, is the secret key that when properly applied allows us to attain Self-realization.

Instead of allowing our attention to focus on an endless stream of objects of perception (including thoughts, feelings, or the body), we need to turn attention in on itself so that awareness becomes aware of itself. The pivoting of our attention inward—referred to by various names such as "attention falling on itself," "awareness resting in awareness," "tracing the mind back to its source," or simply "watching the 'I am'"—refers to the practice of working directly with awareness. This shift in focus captures the essence of what Sri Ramana, Sri Nisargadatta, and other liberated sages have taught as the means for attaining Self-awareness.

It goes without saying that terms such as "becoming aware of awareness" do not imply that there are two awarenesses, or two Selves, one searching for the other. There is, of course, only one singular awareness that appears to be searching for itself as long as it is misidentified with the body and mind. So long as duality is present in our consciousness, we will feel that we are a person (one entity) searching for the Self (another entity). But such a false paradigm persists only as long as consciousness is under the influence of *māyā*. The term "awareness resting in awareness" simply denotes the non-dual consciousness becoming aware of itself devoid of any limiting adjuncts such as the body and mind. In other words, the power of knowing, which is consciousness itself, regains its pure state when it is able to know itself to the exclusion of all objects (Vedanta) or, viewed from another angle, when it is able to know and experience everything as non-different from itself (Shaivism).

How our power of attention functions is not difficult to understand: in our present state of bondage, Awareness is identified with a body and mind due to the operation of the ego. Feeling that we are a body, our attention naturally flows out toward objects of perception, and our attraction to sense objects (as well as our desire to avoid them) is what keeps the thought stream flowing. In this way, as long as our attention is pointed outward, our thoughts and perceptions will forever multiply because our sustained attention is what gives them strength. And as long as our thought stream remains strong, so will our identification to the body and mind.

Sadhu Om employs an apt analogy: if you move a film screen away from the projector, the picture grows larger, but if you move the screen closer to the projector, its source of light, the picture becomes smaller until it reduces to the size of a dot. In the same way, the more the lens of our attention is focused outward on our thoughts, the more they multiply and the stronger they become. Conversely, the more our attention is focused inward toward the innate feeling of I, which is the source of the mind's light, the weaker the thought current becomes (that is, the number of thoughts begin to decrease).[38] In the same way, our identification with the body and mind become proportionately weaker as our thought stream thins out. Finally, when the mind becomes utterly quiescent as a result of a sustained and prolonged focus on our I-consciousness, the latter easily dissolves into actual pure Awareness. The entire current of thoughts, which until now seemed unstoppable, comes to an end in a natural way.

Someone once expressed to Sri Ramana their fear that thoughts are so constant, they can never be silenced. He responded as follows:

> You fancy that there is no end if one goes on rejecting every thought when it rises. No. There is an end. If you are vigilant, and make a stern effort to reject every thought when it rises, you will soon find that you are going deeper and deeper into your own inner self. At that level it is not necessary to make an effort to reject thoughts.[39]

The insight here is that the only reason the thought stream appears unbreakable is because we invest it with unlimited energy by fueling it with our power of attention. If we think about it, we rarely if ever shift our attention away from objects of perception. We are always keen to witness one thought or another, or to observe one thing or another, never stopping to focus on the raw feeling that we exist. It is the constant tendency of the mind to grasp at things other than itself that is responsible for keeping us spinning in the wheel of *saṃsāra* (the repeated cycle of birth and death).

In this light, struggling to suppress thoughts is a recipe for disaster. Fighting thoughts or wrestling against thoughts necessitates paying attention to thoughts, which has the

---

38. Sri Sadhu Om, *The Path of Sri Ramana: Part One* (Tiruvannamalai: Sri Ramana Kshetra, Kanvashrama Trust, 1971).
39. Godman, *Be As You Are.*

unintended effect of empowering them. Wrestling with thoughts is no different than trying to hold a spring down by pressing it. The very act of pushing down invests the spring with the energy it needs to rise up. In the same way, wrestling with thoughts only strengthens them. Instead, the secret to dissolving the mind into pure Awareness is to turn our attention away from the thought stream (and the external world) and focus it like a laser beam on the first person singular feeling, our knowing subject.

What we fail to realize is that our I-consciousness is the very Self we are seeking. Even though in its present condition our I-consciousness is mixed up with the feeling of being a body, by focusing on our sense of being, it becomes possible to attain the Self. As Sadhu Om says, "Attention is attachment," and as humans we have the ability to direct our attention toward the body-mind or toward the formless Self.[40] As long as the attention is directed outward toward objects, the act of attending to objects is by definition a "doing," while pivoting the attention inward to rest on our innate sense of being is not a "doing" but a "being."[41] Attention that rests on itself is no different than being still or attaining silence (in the technical sense of the word).[42] In this way, Self-attention results in Self-realization.

The power of attention, then, is a ray of light emitted from the Self that illumines the way back to the Self. It is actually the manifestation of God's grace within every human being, for whatever receives our attention eventually becomes a reality. If we focus all our attention on something—whether it be a goal or a physical object—it will inevitably manifest

40. Sri Sadhu Om, *Path of Sri Ramana*.
41. Ibid.
42. Here silence does not refer to an absence of sounds, but to remaining centered in thoughtless Awareness, where only non-dual Consciousness prevails.

as long as both the intensity and duration of attention are sufficiently strong.[43]

The phenomenon of child prodigies serves as a great example. The child's intense attention to their art or science carried on uninterruptedly throughout their previous lives carries forth into the present incarnation, suddenly yielding its complete fruit. Although it appears as if the child is able to perform at exceptional levels out of thin air, the reality is that they have been focusing their attention on their craft for years and years. Likewise, if we turn our attention inward toward our own sense of being, we will in due course attain the most worthy and coveted of attainments, which is none other than the Self's infinite peace and bliss.

Finally, it is equally important to understand that simply locating our pure Awareness is not enough. Once we locate it (which is what is defined as making contact with the Self), we have to keep returning to it, while at the same time reminding ourselves that Awareness is our true nature and that our body and mind are but specks of dust floating within that blissful and vast expanse of Consciousness.

Sadhu Om's Objections Regarding Traditional Practices

In order to drive home the point that nothing other than our innate I-consciousness should serve as the target of our attention, Sadhu Om goes so far as to speak out against four

---

43. This is why the so-called Law of Attraction is an incomplete teaching. In the Law of Attraction, constantly thinking about something is supposed to materialize it in a short amount of time. What is missing from the teaching is that due to the multitude of thoughts occurring in an ordinary mind, each thought is extremely weak, which means the mind has no power to attract or materialize what it is contemplating unless it thinks about it for a very long time. Only a mind that has become strong and one-pointed through yogic practices is capable of giving rise to thoughts that are powerful enough to attract or materialize what is being contemplated within a moment, a few days, or a few years.

traditional and time-honored practices that have been relied on for centuries. Our purpose in reviewing his concerns is to help shed further light on the subtle mechanics of yoga.

Specifically, he takes issue with (1) witness-based meditation practices such as *vipassanā* (insight); (2) repetition of *mahāvākya*-type statements such as "I am That," "I am Shiva," or "everything is Consciousness"; (3) engaging in classic *neti, neti* (not this, not this) analysis; and (4) the practice of *japa* (mental repetition of a mantra).[44] A brief outline of each practice is given below, followed by a summary of Sadhu Om's objections.

Vipassanā: One method of practicing *sati* (mindfulness) or "witness consciousness" is to observe all cognitions and perceptions with a detached mind. Thoughts, emotions, aches and pains, the sounds from across the street, the flow of the breath—all of these are to be observed without any sense of entanglement. By calm, detached observation, the witnessing part of the mind, i.e., our consciousness, is able to establish a gap between itself and what is being observed, and the awareness of the gap is what allows our I-feeling to begin to recognize itself as pure, formless Consciousness.

Mahāvākyas: Repetitions of high level, expansive thoughts such as "everything is consciousness," "I am Shiva," "I am That," or "the universe exists within me" are Tantric practices designed to expand the yogin's sense of identity beyond the perimeter of the body and mind to include all of creation. By contemplating the entire universe as moving within one's field of awareness, the ego is purified until one's actual experience of oneself as pure Consciousness begins to take hold.

Neti, neti: In the practice of *neti, neti*, a meditator takes every object he can observe and affirms that because it is observable, it cannot be who he really is. This traditional method of negation is designed to deliver the practitioner into a state of witness consciousness. For example, we can

44. Sri Sadhu Om, *Path of Sri Ramana*.

46

begin by affirming that we are not the room we are sitting in. Next, we can consider our body and the fact that if we lose a limb, we will nevertheless continue to feel that we exist as the same person, implying that our body cannot be the source of our true identity. Likewise, if we compare ourselves as a child to the adult we are now, we will find that almost nothing has remained the same. Every cell in our body has changed, as well as the quality of the thoughts flowing through our mind. And yet, despite a constantly changing body and mind, we have never stopped feeling that we are the same person. The inescapable conclusion is that the continuity of our being is able to persist because it is the innate Consciousness within which is the true repository of our identity, and not the transient body or mind. When we strip away and discard all the layers we normally take ourselves to be, we awake to the realization that only Consciousness remains.

Japa: The practice of *japa* is defined as the silent repetition of a mantra. The mantra can be repeated during our formal meditation session or while we go about our daily routine. Although mantras can be repeated in various ways, the most prescribed method is to join the mantra to the breath, harmonizing one repetition to the inbreath and one repetition to the outbreath. Since the mantra takes the form of a thought, at its most superficial level the mantra prevents other thoughts from flooding the mind (the mind can only think one thought at a time, although the progression between thoughts is lightning fast), which allows the mind to grow strong in concentration. As the mind becomes one-pointed, it is able to hold the mantra before it like a flame that does not flicker, and the total fusion of attention into the mantra causes the mind to lose awareness of itself as a separate observer or knower. Put differently, our I-ness or ego becomes absorbed in the mantra, which allows the mind to enter into the lower stages of *samādhi*.

Since each of the above methods are time-honored yogic practices, why does Sadhu Om speak against them? With regard to *vipassanā*, Sadhu Om's view is that watching thoughts, the breath, or objects of perception, even with a detached mind, will never reveal the Self. As long as we watch thoughts, we commit the double error of keeping our attention away from our I-feeling as well as empowering the very thoughts we are trying to get rid of.

As for the *mahāvākyas*, in Sadhu Om's view repeating statements such as, "everything is consciousness," or "I am Shiva," does not amount to anything. Because such utterances are mere conceptual thoughts, they will never have the power to reveal the Self. Instead, the *mahāvākya* is simply the conclusion we arrive at *after* becoming established in Self-awareness. It is not a method to attain the Self. The mistake is akin to repeating, "I am in Rome, I am in Rome," before we have even made the effort to drive to the airport, get on a plane, and fly to Rome. Just as invoking the destination does not amount to making the trip, in the same way repeating "I am Shiva" in a superficial and mechanical way can never result in Self-awareness.

Regarding the practice of *neti, neti*, Sadhu Om points out that while the method of negation tells you what you are not, it fails to take the further step of conveying the right practice or technique to attain the Self. In other words, understanding that we are not the body or the mind is only a first and necessary step that opens the door to actual spiritual practice.[45] Otherwise, we can repeat a thousand times to ourselves that we are not the body-mind, but if we do not take any further action, then of what use is such knowledge?

Finally, *japa*, or mantra repetition, is felled by the same arguments applied to the practices of *vipassanā* and the *mahāvākyas*. Since a mantra is a thought (albeit a very pure and powerful thought), Sadhu Om argues that as an object of perception, a mantra can never lead the mind into the actual silence and stillness of Self-awareness.

45. Ibid.

Despite this, Sadhu Om is at least willing to concede that mantra repetition is effective in making the mind one-pointed, which helps sustain the long periods of Self-attention required of the mind once it is directed inward. Yet, because in his view mantra repetition in and of itself does nothing to shift our attention inward toward our sense of being, he believes it may ultimately cause more harm than good.[46] In contrast, bringing the mind to rest directly on the I-feeling not only causes it to become one-pointed, it does so with a mind that is already inward facing.

A further concession Sadhu Om is willing to offer is that when a mantra is repeated with heart-melting love for God or Guru, the love felt by the seeker indicates that he or she is actually following the path of devotion (*bhakti-mārga*), which is, at least at the surface level, a different path from Self-enquiry and the only alternative approach that Sri Ramana was willing to endorse.[47]

As a point of comparison, it is interesting to note that Patañjali in his *Yoga Sūtra* teaches the very opposite: he teaches that for the I-consciousness to become aware of itself, the yogin must pass through many levels of *samādhi*, and the journey always begins by focusing on an object of perception, such as a mantra, and not directly on the I-feeling. According to Patañjali, the beginner's mind is not subtle enough to latch directly onto the I-consciousness, so a beginner should start by focusing on an appropriate object of perception. As steadiness of mind improves, the objects before the mind become increasingly subtle, until the power of attention is finally able to move past all objects of perception, becoming aware of itself.[48]

46. Ibid.
47. Ibid. Sri Ramana was fully aware that on final analysis, heart-melting love for the Self and complete attention on the Self amount to one and the same thing. The only difference is that Self-attention begins with the mind, while devotion begins with the heart.
48. See *Yoga Sūtra*, 1:17 and 1:18.

In response to Patañjali, Sri Ramana states that any type of *samādhi* gained by merging into an object external to the Self will only result in a mere abeyance of the mind, and will not result in the mind's irrevocable destruction.[49] In all of the *samādhis* taught by Patañjali (except his last two: *nirbīja samādhi* and *dharma-megha samādhi*), the mind is plunged into a state of *laya* (abeyance) in which the deep *vāsanas* (latent mental tendencies and impressions) remain intact. When such a mind rises from *samādhi*, the ego rises along with it, and one's limited existence resumes.[50] It is for this reason that Sri Ramana teaches that focusing on our I-feeling from the onset is the fastest approach. According to Sadhu Om's view, there is no reason to consider our mind so weak as to be unfit to focus on the I-feeling that is already with us, and there is nothing to be gained by taking the circuitous route of concentrating on objects of perception that are external to our formless, motionless Awareness.

Qualifying Sadhu Om's Teachings

While Sadhu Om's arguments against the four yogic practices raise important and legitimate points, I believe his teachings leave room for qualification and that the traditional practices of *japa*, repeating *mahāvākyas*, *neti*, *neti*, and so forth, when done in the right way, can significantly help bring us closer to Self-awareness. This is particularly true for aspirants who at first are unable to identify or sustain a direct connection with their I-consciousness.

Specifically, Sadhu Om's concerns should only be understood to apply when the practice in question is being performed in an externalized or mechanical way. To practice them properly, it is best to apply a Vedantic perspective to *vipassanā* and *neti*, *neti*, and a Tantric perspective to *japa* and

49. Godman, *Be As You Are.*
50. Ibid.

the *mahāvākyas*. As we have seen, any method that tries to separate or disentangle creation from pure Consciousness qualifies as Vedantic, while any method that tries to recognize an object of perception as pure Consciousness is Tantric in nature. (This is an oversimplification, but it suits our purposes.)

Taking *vipassanā* as an example, if we observe thoughts mechanically, nothing will be gained, but if we passively observe thoughts with a high level of awareness, not only are we able to detect the separation between our awareness and our thoughts (which disempowers our thoughts), but more importantly, we are able to create an opening that allows us to turn our attention toward the Self. The key point here is to observe thoughts with conscious awareness, or with bare attention, since, as the Buddhist monk Bhante Gunaratana points out, being *aware* of a thought is very different than just *thinking* a thought.[51] In the former, we know a thought is passing before the screen of our mind, while in the latter we are completely and unconsciously joined to the thought. And as we know, thoughts obscure Self-awareness. The same logic applies to the practice of *neti, neti*, where we practice observing all objects of perception as foreign to us, until we are able to experience ourselves as pure Consciousness.

On the other hand, the practices of *japa* and repeating *mahāvākyas* lend themselves to a Tantric approach. In other words, instead of looking upon objects of perception as separate from us, we must view them as expressions of our own consciousness, which ultimately enables us to penetrate into the Awareness that underlies both us and the object.

Taking mantra repetition as an example, when we are able to invoke the feeling that the mantra, its meaning, and the person repeating the mantra are a unified consciousness, at that very moment the mantra begins to unfold with full force, purifying our body and mind and initiating many yogic

---

51. Bhante Gunaratana, *Mindfulness in Plain English* (Boston: Wisdom Publications, 2011).

processes. (If we are having trouble understanding how the syllables of a mantra are in reality pure Consciousness, we can think of how the various images on a movie screen are nothing but a single beam of light.) In this way, we should be able to arrive at the experience that the mantra is repeating itself, or that it is the Self who repeats the mantra. Put differently, what we need to get rid of is the feeling that we, a person, are repeating a mantra, an object. This is what keeps the mantra powerless, and it is this kind of mechanical and dualistic repetition that is the target of Sadhu Om's criticism.

At first, trying to identify all objects as Consciousness is simply a vague feeling born of intellectual understanding. But as time goes by, we will actually begin to experience that both we and the object in question are made up of nothing but Consciousness. The knowing that arises is not intellectual but empirical, and its arrival marks one of the greatest moments in our lives.

When it comes to the vibration of a mantra, the pulsation of Shakti within it makes it extremely powerful and effective. And since the entire universe is really an emission of subtle vibration, mantric syllables offer immediate access to the Self in a way that, perhaps for a seeker in the early stages of practice, focusing on our I-consciousness cannot. Since ordinary thought waves are in essence vibrations of sound, fighting sound with sound can be as effective as fighting fire with fire.

When we repeat a mantra, there are three important considerations to keep in mind: the actual vibration of sound, the meaning of the words, and the inner feeling behind each repetition.

With regard to a mantra's vibration, a mantra is not a random collection of sounds but a gross, articulated version of the subtle vibrations heard by the inner ear of enlightened beings absorbed in meditation. The vibrations of "aum" or "om" in the inner ear, for example, have the natural ability to quiet the mind and unfold the full power of Awareness (as opposed to exciting the mind in the way that other groups of sounds are capable of doing). Moreover, mantras that have been accepted and repeated over thousands of years are invested with the energy of all the minds who repeated them (we call this lineage energy). Mantras such as *Om Namaḥ Shivāya, Om Namo Nārāyaṇāya, Om Sai Ram, Ram, Om Guru Om,* or *So'ham* (heard beneath the breath as "so-hum"), among many others that have been passed down from Guru to disciple, literally carry the power and energy of all the saints who repeated them.

Incidentally, there is much discussion within yogic circles regarding what kinds of mantras are effective. Some believe that only a mantra received from a living Guru carries any power, while mantras picked up from books or audio recordings are essentially dead. While there is no doubt that the most efficacious mantras come from authentic living Masters who have infused them with their own power, in my view, mantras heard or read can also be effective as long as they are repeated with proper technique and feeling. Although these mantras may take longer to reveal their power, the force of our own attention and devotion will enable them to initiate numerous yogic processes.

The second consideration regarding mantra repetition pertains to the meaning of the mantra. Unlike ordinary words such as "car," "apple," "chair," etc., which point to external objects of perception, mantras always point inwardly toward our own Self. *Om Namaḥ Shivāya,* for example, means "I bow to or honor Lord Shiva," which is another way of saying, "I bow to or honor my own Self." So even though the mantra appears at first as a separate object that stands before our awareness, the sound itself is inward facing insofar as its meaning and its vibrations point back to the Self. This is another reason why the mind easily grows calm under the influence of a mantra.

Finally, and more importantly, the inner feeling (our *bhāva*) behind each mantra repetition is what separates success from failure. Above all, it is vital to understand that the sound form of the mantra is not a symbol that points to the inner Self, but rather *is* the Self in sound form. This Tantric realization, which is not easy to arrive at, is the secret key that unlocks the power of the mantra. Moreover, because the sound body of the mantra is in fact the Self, and because we have identified our I-consciousness as the Self, the understanding that the mantra and our I-feeling are exactly the same is the final element that enables the mantra to dissolve our mind into pure Consciousness. Otherwise, as long as we feel that the reciter and the object of recitation are separate entities, we will gain little beyond a calming effect on the mind, even if we repeat our mantra a million times. As with everything in *sādhanā*, the secret lies in bringing proper awareness into the practice. Once we associate the mantra to our I-feeling, we are able to repeat it with great love and affection.

In this light, it comes as no surprise that Sri Ramana takes a softer view than Sadhu Om when it comes to the value of working with secondary objects of perception, such as a mantra, the image of the Guru, or the breath. Specifically, while both Sri Ramana and Sadhu Om agree that focusing on objects of perception of any kind can never serve as a *direct* path to the Self, Sri Ramana accepts that there is no harm in resorting to an indirect path if the mind is at first unable to make lasting contact with its I-feeling. Sri Ramana states:

> Meditation differs according to the degree of advancement of the seeker. If one is fit for it one might directly hold on to the thinker [our I-feeling], and the thinker will then automatically sink into its source, pure consciousness. If one cannot directly hold on to the thinker one must meditate on God and in due course the same individual will have become sufficiently pure to hold on to the thinker and to sink into absolute being.[52]

52. Sri Ramana quoted in Godman, *Be As You Are.*

54

To clarify, by "meditate on God," Sri Ramana is referring to a conceptual form of God held in thought or image.

Nevertheless, Sadhu Om makes a necessary point when he reminds us that if our minds remain completely externalized, then any practice we undertake will also remain mechanical and superficial, yielding limited results. Since with a little guidance it is not difficult to turn our attention directly toward our innate I-consciousness, in Sadhu Om's view there is no need to rely on intermediary mechanisms.

CHAPTER FOUR

Exactly Who Attains Liberation?

If zeroing in on our I-consciousness forms the basis of practice, the next step is to consider exactly who or what attains liberation. On the one hand we have a physical body, which is only a lump of flesh that is insentient and incapable of performing any *sādhanā*, while on the other hand we have pure Awareness which requires no spiritual practice as it is already perfect. That leaves us with the mind, which as we have already seen is composed of thoughts, perceptions, intellect, and ego, and which rises between the Self and the body. And yet tradition also classifies the mind as insentient given that its appearance as conscious is only due to the light of Awareness cast onto it, much in the way that the moon is only able to shine by the reflected light of the sun. This begs the question: If, like the body, the mind is not even conscious, then who stands to benefit from liberation?

From one perspective, it is wrong to conceive of any particular entity becoming liberated. After all, the Self is immutable and beyond bondage and liberation. The mind, for its part, is a created object that can never contain the Self, just as a teacup cannot contain the ocean.

In this view, the appearance of the ego creates the impression that pure Awareness is wrongly identified to the body and mind. (I say impression since the Self is never truly bound.) A balance is struck between the knowing subject and the object perceived, meaning that we (the ego) feel ourselves to be both the body-mind as well as the consciousness within it. In other words, the rise of the limited I-sense creates the experience that a little of the Self has mixed with the body-mind and a little of the body-mind has mixed with the Self. (Consider slightly overlapping blue and yellow circles and the resulting green shape which rises in the middle.) An equilibrium is established by the ego that allows the triad of knower, knowledge, and known to persist, and as long as the division is maintained our I-sense prevails. Once the ego is purified or destroyed, the Self's indirect association to the mind and body fall away, meaning that the phantom I-sense dissolves. Accordingly, under this model there is no actual entity that becomes liberated aside from the phantom I-consciousness. The moment the latter dissolves, pure Awareness rests in itself. (This is the perspective favored by Sri Ramana.)

Alternatively, another point of view suggests that it is the intellect itself that becomes enlightened. In this view, it is not the Self that appears to misidentify to the body-mind through the agency of the ego, but the intellect (which neatly resolves the conundrum of how an eternally unchanging Self can become seemingly misidentified to an object of knowledge [the body-mind], which implies change).

As we have already learned, the intellect acts like a mirror that continuously reflects to the Self what the other parts of the mind are presenting to it. When the mind is stilled, the intellect is left with nothing to reflect back to the Self, and emptied of all content, the intellect is purified to the point of "transparency" so that it only reflects the light of the Self which illumines it in the first place. Stillness of mind causes the ego to collapse, and freed from the ego's limiting influence which forced it to identify with the thought-flux and other objects of perception, the intellect is said to achieve Self-realization insofar as it remains filled exclusively with awareness of nothing but the Self. Verse 9 of Abhinavagupta's *Paramārthasāra* states:

As a face shines forth in a spotlessly clean mirror, in the same way the supreme lord who is of the nature of illumination shines forth in the *buddhi tattva* (intellect) that has been purified following the descent of divine grace by the Lord.[53]

Specifically, the intellect that is the recipient of *shaktipāt* becomes purified from the limiting influence of the *ānava*, *māyīya*, and *kārma malas* which obscure it. In Vedanta, the purification of the intellect is not framed against the three *malas*, which are central to Kashmir Shaivism, but from the impurities that flow from the three *gunas*. Swami Vishnu Tirth Maharaj puts it this way:

Realization of *Ātman*, *Ishwar* or *Guru-tattwa*, by whatever name we may choose to call it, appears in the *buddhi* of the aspirant, purified of all the impurities born of *tamo-guna* and *rajoguna*, like an image in a clear mirror quite distinctly.[54]

When the enlightened yogin rises from his final meditation session, the mind's cognitions and thought stream are again reflected in the intellect, but the absence of the ego allows the intellect to remain exclusively identified with the pure Awareness that stands behind it. It is important to note that identification with pure Awareness also implies identification with all objects in existence, since the entire universe is felt to be contained with one's awareness. Put differently,

---

53. Deba Brata SenSharma, trans., *Paramārthasāra of Abhinavagupta: Essence of the Supreme Truth* (New Delhi: Muktabodha Indological Research Institute, 2007).
54. Swami Vishnu Tirth Maharaj, *Devātmā śakti: Kundalini Divine Power* (Rishikesh: Yoga Sri Peeth, 1974).

enlightenment does not mean that the body will no longer be perceived. The body will still be considered part of oneself, but instead of being felt as the sole totality of our being, the body will simply remain as one object among many that we consider to be "us," just as we consider all of our ten fingers to be equally part of us.

Throughout the intellect's entire process of moving from impure to pure, or from bound to liberated, the Self remains as an unaffected witness. In other words, it makes no difference to the Self whether the intellect is misidentified with the mind and body or properly identified to the Self. Full and final absorption into pure Awareness only transpires when the yogin passes away, causing the intellect to sink once and for all back into its source.

Accordingly, both models differ in that under the first one, it is the Self (through the appearance of the phantom I-sense) that becomes seemingly misidentified to the body-mind, while in the second, it is the intellect proper that is considered the victim of misidentification.

It bears mentioning that the above perspectives are not necessarily mutually exclusive. In fact, they can both be considered correct insofar as the collapse of the phantom I-sense is what enables the intellect to directly cognize the Self. In this way, one follows the other, which allows us to say that liberation belongs both to the Self (indirectly through the death of the limited I-sense) as well as to the intellect, which is the only part of the mind capable of directly reflecting the Self.

It is also helpful to keep in mind that the above discussion is purely academic, and while metaphysical models can convey a sense of clarity and stability, they do nothing in terms of furthering our realization of the Self. For this reason, it makes no difference in terms of practice whether we prefer one version over the other, given that the moment we focus our attention on our I-sense, we sidestep the thought process altogether. Only awareness resting in awareness grants final Self-realization, and the proof lies in the fact that yogins from directly opposing traditions attain equally excellent *samādhi*. At the end of the day, the final truth regarding such matters will only reveal itself to us when we become established in our own Self-awareness.

Working with the Mind

Since we have identified the ego as the primary culprit behind our limited awareness, and given that the ego will never eliminate itself, how can the mind manage to get rid of the ego? Sri Ramana states:

> To ask the mind to kill the mind is like making the thief the policeman. He will go with you and pretend to catch the thief, but nothing will be gained. So you must turn inward and see from where the mind rises and then it will cease to exist.[55]

In other words, even if we conceptually think about the Self all day long, offer the fruits of our actions to God, or pretend that we have no ego, it will not result in any Self-realization. And yet, while it appears impossible for the mind to transcend itself, there is in fact a way out of the conundrum, which is to set the entire mind aside through the power of attention. As Sri Ramana reveals above, ignoring our body and mind altogether by shifting our attention onto our I-feeling is the direct method of attainment. And since the ability to focus and guide the power of attention is under the sway of the mind, attaining Self-awareness is not something we have to sit around and passively wait for.

Sri Ramana's teaches us to ask ourselves "Who am I?" But his teaching is greatly misunderstood, since the instruction can create the impression that the question is to be answered by another thought. Yet Sri Ramana was not expecting us to

55. Godman, *Be As You Are*.

come up with another discursive thought to answer "Who am I?" Instead, asking "Who am I?" was intended to lead our attention directly into our pure I-feeling. In other words, silent Self-attention is the right answer to the inquiry, "Who am I?"

That said, the reason why so many have misunderstood Sri Ramana's method of Self-enquiry is because to arrive at Self-attention after asking "Who am I?" or "Who is the thinker?" requires a pre-existing intellectual understanding that we are neither the body or the mind. Only after we have identified our innate I-feeling as the center of awareness can we practice Self-enquiry correctly.

In fact, practicing Self-enquiry is so simple the technique is liable to be missed. If we recall the exercise of throwing our attention around from our big toe to our ear, we see how easy it is to shift our attention from one thing to another. Likewise, it is just as easy to shift our attention inward, allowing it to rest on our natural feeling of being. The problem, of course, is that our attention will only remain on itself for very short periods of time (seconds in fact), before it is pulled back into the rushing current of thoughts. So the logical next question is to ask how to keep our attention focused on our I-feeling for extended periods of time.

Surprisingly, the answer lies in taking help from the primary obstacle obscuring the Self: our thought stream. Since we are presently so closely identified with the mind, we have no choice but to depend on thought as a pointing mechanism to guide our attention back in on itself. For example, as soon as we realize we are in the grip of thoughts, we can insert a new thought to return our attention to our innate sense of being, such as, "Who is the witness to all these thoughts?" or "I should refocus on my I-feeling." By asking "Who is the thinker?" or by remembering that pure Awareness is the source of all thoughts, we can easily regain the thread of Self-attention. For this reason it is correct to accept that some thoughts can be liberating. In this way, the careful and strategic use of thought to guide our attention back onto itself is akin to using a stick to stir a fire until the stick itself is thrown in and consumed by the flames. That is, once our ability to keep our attention on the Self becomes firm through practice, we will no longer need to rely on thoughts to drive us back toward Self-attention. It will become an automatic habit.

Even though our I-feeling at present does not radiate any special feeling of bliss or peace (because it is tainted by the ego), maintaining our focus on our I-feeling will undoubtedly cause the thought-flux and ego to grow weaker until the light of the Self begins to shine through. For this reason, making contact with the Self is actually extremely easy, but because Self-attention does not immediately give rise to any of the qualities we associate with an enlightened mind (peace, bliss, supranormal powers, etc.), the doorway into Self-awareness is easily missed. If we persist with the practice, in time a shift in our identity from being a person to being the pure Self will begin to take hold, along with the accompanying peace and bliss that are the marks of spiritual advancement.

A helpful practice point that Sadhu Om recommends is that each time Self-attention slackens, we should relax the mind for a moment prior to resuming our efforts. In other words, instead of struggling to hold on to our I-feeling without a break, it is better to rest for a moment before coming back to the practice. This is because each isolated attempt at Self-attention delivers a strong force, just as pressing one's thumb on a pressure scale for a short period of time registers a higher reading than holding one's thumb down for a longer period, which actually causes the pressure to slip.[56] So each time we catch ourselves lost in thought, we need only bring our attention back to our I-feeling. As our practice strengthens, we will find that we are able to rest in the Self for longer and longer periods of time.

56. This analogy is Sadhu Om's, not mine. See *Path of Sri Ramana*.

Thoughts Are Both Sticky and Seductive

The principal function of the ego is to make our thoughts "sticky" in the sense that we are hopelessly identified with them. And while we may believe that during our waking state we are quite aware, from the perspective of the Self, our thinking obscures awareness the way dust on a bulb dims its light.

During normal thinking, we are aware of our thoughts but also well aware of our body and our surroundings. However, as we have all experienced, if we suddenly slip into a daydream, then for those few seconds we are only aware of the daydream. But the moment we snap out of our daydream (which is a type of mini awakening), we immediately regain normal awareness of our thoughts, body, and the external world.

From the perspective of the Self, normal thinking is much like being lost in a daydream. There is very little awareness of Awareness. So each time we direct our attention to our I-consciousness, we enable the intellect to identify with pure Awareness much in the same way as when we transition from a daydream back into normal thinking.

An objection can be raised that when we focus our attention on the I-feeling, we still remain quite aware of our body and mind (unlike snapping out of a daydream, which causes the daydream to disappear completely).

Although it is true that attending to our I-feeling does not eliminate our awareness of the mind, body, and world, repeatedly doing so (along with the practice of formal meditation discussed in chapter five) will lead us into the non-dual state of *samādhi* where nothing but pure Awareness is cognized. It is simply a matter of persistent practice before we are able experience ourselves as absolute Consciousness.

In addition to being "sticky," thoughts have another sinister quality: they are quite seductive, causing us to become infatuated with them. If we had no interest in our thoughts, it would be much easier for us to quiet them down. But what a lot of seekers fail to realize is that we are quite in love with our thoughts. In the blink of an eye our imagination takes us to an exciting place, or we relive a memory that brings us joy, or we cannot stop worrying about something. Whether good or bad, thoughts hold our attention captive throughout almost every waking moment. In fact, most of our existence as humans is lived in the realm of imagination and memory and most of us would be terrified at the idea of not living with our thoughts. It is for this very reason that we need to practice Self-attention again and again, until we begin to experience that existing without thoughts is not only peaceful and joyous, but is the essence of happiness.

Naturally, many of us may wonder how we can possibly get through the day if we are constantly shunning our thoughts. How will decisions get made? How will we know where to drive if the thought of our destination does not flash in our mind? As a matter of fact, the very idea of living without thought seems ludicrous at best.

In terms of fulfilling our karma, what needs to be thought of will be thought of and what needs to be done will be done. But since we cough up so many hundreds of useless thoughts per day, there is no cause to worry if we practice eliminating as many as possible as they arise. In fact, the more we reduce thoughts, the sharper our intellect becomes, with each remaining thought growing stronger and stronger.[57] Moreover, as we became anchored in the recognition that we are the Self, many of our actions will happen spontaneously under the inspiration and command of the Self. In the end, enlightenment does not mean the total cessation of thoughts or actions. The latter only occurs during periods of formal

---

57. The often used analogy is that of a wire with a limited amount of electricity connected to a hundred light bulbs. As more and more light bulbs are turned off, more electricity is freed up to flow into each remaining light bulb, causing it to shine that much more brightly.

meditation when we plunge into *nirvikalpa samādhi*. After emerging into the final state of *sahaja samādhi*, the thought stream is still present to guide the body through life, with the primary difference that the intellect of such a mind does not identify in the least with the passing thoughts or body (because the ego has been expunged), but experiences them as a movement within the field of its own consciousness.[58]

Our infatuation with thoughts is a by-product of the ego. But instead of continuing to live in the dull sleep of the waking state, we should practice ignoring our thoughts and centering on our true Self. That is why it is said that a *jñānin* (a Self-aware being) is asleep (centered on the Self) while everyone else is awake, and awake while everyone else is asleep (with an intellect never identified to thoughts). If we aspire to make progress in *sādhanā*, we must begin by letting go of the fear of transcending our thoughts.

58. In the end everything is cognized as consciousness, just as a goldsmith perceives all the bracelets, earrings, rings, and sculptures spread out on his table as nothing but gold.

CHAPTER FIVE

Meditation Instructions

Even though attending to our I-feeling constitutes our core spiritual practice, many of us will find it impossible to sustain an inward gaze throughout an entire day. For this reason, it is vital to supplement our practice with formal meditation (*dhyāna* in Sanskrit). Although Sri Ramana and his leading disciples viewed formal meditation as unnecessary or required only of neophytes, unless we are so spiritually evolved as they were to be able to keep our attention locked on to our I-feeling at all times, we would be wise to consider closed-eyed meditation as the cornerstone of our *sādhanā*.[59] From this perspective, formal meditation becomes the primary practice, with everything else taking on a supporting role.

The attempt to make our mind rest in its own innate awareness is, of course, the very definition of what it means to meditate, and in this way it is no different than watching our I-feeling as we go about our day. However, when we sit with closed eyes, we gain access to a depth of stillness that greatly accelerates our absorption into Self-awareness. As we shall see, many subtle yogic processes unfold during formal meditation, including physical and mental purificatory *kriyās* (spontaneous movements) that primarily express themselves during our closed-eyed practice. Our flight into highly visual states of consciousness, which mark an important stage of

59. See Godman, *Be As You Are.*

progress, can likewise only transpire when we are sitting with our eyes closed, and not, for example, while we are walking around the office. These are just a few reasons why we should never underestimate the value and importance of sitting down to meditate, keeping in mind that our final absorption into the Self will most likely occur during our formal practice.

Attending to our I-feeling during our waking state as well as during our closed-eyed session are mutually complementary, with each one strengthening the other. In this light, if we hope to meditate deeply, we must at other times maintain an effort to practice awareness, further supplementing with mantra repetition, chanting, studying, or any other practices we enjoy. And yet this does not mean that any centering we achieve during the day will compare to the experiences that are bound to manifest during formal meditation. The latter are much greater and more powerful in nature, giving rise to intense states of bliss, peace, and divine knowledge, as our energies become collected and one-pointed.

Some meditation teachers take great pride in emphasizing that their technique does not involve any act of concentration, any form of mental control or manipulation, or any effort whatsoever, making it sound as if there is absolutely nothing to be done and that the secret of practice lies somehow in the effortless aspect of the technique. Yet, when we are taught such techniques, a mantra will invariably be imparted with instructions to repeat it without any strain or stress, simply allowing the energy of the mantra do all the work. Alternatively, the student may be instructed to passively witness thoughts or the breath as commonly found in the practice of mindfulness.

While the promise of an entirely effortless technique may sound appealing, as long as our sense of being is fused to the thought stream that populates our mind, some form of effort, however subtle, will be needed to allow awareness to become aware of itself. For example, even if we are only practicing mindfulness (where our attention is simply observing what is passing before it), to remain aware of ourselves as a detached witness is an act of knowledge that must be continuously refreshed, since our attention will invariably be dragged back into our thoughts. Similarly, even if we are just repeating a mantra, the very act of repetition and of gently bringing our attention back to the mantra when other thoughts crowd it out is also a form of effort. Likewise, ignoring thoughts and fixing our attention exclusively on our I-feeling also requires a sustained effort, however gentle it may be.

Accordingly, even when practicing the most "passive" forms of meditation, there must be a degree of alert attention, which of course is another word for effort (otherwise we will remain lost in the sleep of thoughts, which is our normal state of affairs). For this reason, we would do well to be wary when we come across promises of entirely effortless meditation techniques; for as long as thoughts are present in the mind, effort of one kind or another simply cannot be avoided.

With this in mind, there is nothing to fear when we come across the word "effort," for without right effort, nothing in yoga can be accomplished (unless Lord Shiva decides to elevate us through an impromptu act of grace). As a matter of fact, we can be thankful that as humans we possess the self-awareness, intelligence, and willpower to be able to direct our thoughts and attention in a meaningful way.

As with most things, effective meditation requires not merely a casual effort but the full investment of our hearts and minds. Only the right effort can produce the desired result, and though there are many valid approaches to meditation, the practices and instructions discussed below are the ones which I personally have found to be supremely effective. So let us dive headlong into the ocean of auspiciousness—that supreme jewel of yoga which is the glorious and nectar-filled practice of meditation.

Preparing for Meditation

Firming Our Resolve

Meditation actually begins each night before we retire to bed, for it is then that we affirm our intention to sacrifice some sleep for the sake of our practice. When the alarm rings, we can wake with a sense of excitement and anticipation for the upcoming session. In other words, our practice should never feel like a chore. Normally though, we tend to get excited about things that bring us immediate happiness or pleasure; so until the natural peace and bliss that emanate from making contact with the Self begins to flow (which can take some time), what is needed is a strong sense of commitment in the same way that a marathon runner commits to training at all costs. If we are serious about making progress, we can take a vow to meditate every day, allowing for interruptions only when we fall sick or when we find ourselves in the midst of unexpected circumstances that make it impossible for us to sit for our session.

A firm resolve to meditate every day, seven days a week, actually opens us up to the power of God's grace, and as many of us can attest, the moment we establish a firm intention, the universe conspires to assist us. As a matter of fact, meditation is considered to be the highest form of worship, and as Sri Ramana used to say, our perseverance is the only true sign of our progress.[60]

Time, Place, and Objects of Practice

The time and place of meditation matter. As much as possible, we should try to meditate at the same time every day, ideally in the early hours of the morning just before dawn. The hours between 3:00 and 6:00 a.m. are particularly effective due to the natural silence found in the environment as well as the fact that our thought cycle has not yet kicked into high gear,

---

60. Sri Ramana quoted in James, *Happiness and the Art of Being*.

i.e., our minds are naturally calm. That said, there was a period of time where I meditated from 6:00 to 7:00 a.m., and I found that hour to be equally effective. Meditation beyond this time frame proves increasingly challenging, since the thought-flux begins to enter into its active cycle.

One of the most immediate obstacles to meditation that we face is the strong desire to delay getting up as soon as the alarm rings. We like to hit the snooze button, and if we have not had a proper amount of sleep, the tendency to want to sleep for another few minutes can quickly derail our meditation routine. For this reason we should train ourselves to bolt upright the moment our alarm rings (mental strategies such as imagining our Guru standing at the foot of our bed with a stick in hand may help). That said, if on occasion we do not rise at exactly the same time, causing us to begin our session a few minutes late, we should not waste energy fretting over it.

After rising, we should shower to wash away the *tamasic* (inert) energy of sleep. If showering is not possible, at the very least we should wash our face and sprinkle a few drops of water over the crown of our head. Next, we should drink a few sips of water to moisten our throat (I keep a jug of water next to my meditation seat to avoid having to walk down to the kitchen).

It is also helpful to keep a set of clothes reserved only for our practice. Outside of the hottest summer months, I prefer to meditate with a thin woolen sweater as body temperature drops when the muscles relax. More importantly, we should wear pants that are very thin, so as to not obstruct our blood flow. Since we will be sitting for long periods of time, the aim is to reduce the chances of the legs falling asleep, which is both painful and distracting. To this end, I wear a set of fine silk Thai fisherman pants. I also have a few pairs of traditional Indian cotton pants that work well. The point is that the cloth should be very thin and comfortable. Finally, I also like to wear socks, although it's simply a matter of personal preference.

The space we set aside for our practice is of vital importance. We should be able to set aside a small area in the corner of a room that otherwise remains undisturbed. Ideally, we should sit over a rug, since it is important to isolate our body from grass, earth, metal, wood, or cold stone, for all these tend to draw into the ground the spiritual energy we accumulate as we meditate. This is the reason why we see pictures of saints sitting on tiger or deer skins. Sitting over an animal skin symbolizes dominion or lordship over all of nature, but it also acts as an insulating barrier between the meditator's body and the earth.

The idea that we accumulate Shakti as we progress in meditation is not a matter of fancy or romantic idealism. I can personally attest that after meditating intensely for a few months, I noticed white light pulsating from all the pores in my body. At night, after turning out the lights, my entire room would be filled with a strobing white light which my eyes could see as it shot out of my body. When I looked at my hands and in particular my feet, I observed streams of white light flowing from them. During my actual meditation sessions, my body would become highly charged, as if surrounded by an electrical field, to the point where I could actually feel the energy flowing through my nostrils. If I tried to open my eyes, they would burn strongly in response to the Shakti that enveloped me. Sometimes, after ending my session, I would sit quietly noticing a fragrance similar to the smell of roses permeating my body.

As I stated earlier, I share these and other experiences only to make the point that the blessings we receive from a sustained practice are real. The wisdom of the scriptures is authentic, and if we are able to understand that meditation is much more than a mundane exercise to help relax the mind, all the wonder and astonishment that is presently hidden from sight will be ours to experience.

Meditation Cushion

In addition to a rug, I strongly believe that it is best to sit on a cushion as proper posture, alignment, and lower back support are essential if we are to sit comfortably with a straight back for several hours. In fact, the meditation cushion is so important that our practice can completely fail if we do not take care of this one small detail. In order to sit cross-legged for long stretches of time, we need to elevate our hips a few degrees above our knees, and the best way to achieve this is by using a cushion. When we place our hips higher than our knees, it creates a natural incline, which in turn allows our knees to effortlessly touch the ground. Otherwise, if we sit directly on the floor, our hips will be level to our knees, causing the latter to "float" or point up into the air. This is to be avoided as it places a heavy strain on the lower back and will quickly thwart our ability to meditate. Ultimately, we should be able to sit between one to two hours in perfect comfort, and keeping our knees touching the ground is essential.

Finally, to achieve a proper posture, the cushion cannot be too high or too low. A cushion that is too high will create the sensation of falling over when we enter into certain stages of meditation, while one that is too low will not allow us to achieve the desired incline. In my case, I use a cushion that measures 16.5 inches in length, 11 inches in width, 2 inches in depth, and which is filled with buckwheat hulls. The point is that the cushion should adjust and mold to our body, and since each body is different, the size and shape of the cushions will vary. Before choosing this cushion, I tried six or seven others; it is key to take time to experiment until we discover what works for us.

In addition to our cushion, we can also place a foam square between our lower back and the wall to further stabilize our posture. I find sitting against the wall helpful, although it may interfere with certain yogic *kriyās* that cause our body or head to thrust backward.

Posture

Once we have established a comfortable posture that allows us to hold a straight back for a prolonged period of time, we need to find a comfortable way of crossing our legs. Crossing of the legs as well as touching our thumbs to our index fingers in *chin mudrā* is important because it allows the meditative energy to circulate throughout the body, as opposed to letting it exit through the limbs.

Personally, I have always meditated in *ardha padmāsana*, or half-lotus posture. Unless we are experienced *hatha* yogins, it is not necessary to spend three months struggling to perfect a full-lotus posture. With only very small adjustments, I find that it is relatively easy to sit for one to three hours in a half-lotus posture. To achieve a half-lotus, we simply rest our right foot over our left thigh, tucking in the legs. The left leg and foot remain on the carpet.

If for whatever reason half-lotus proves too uncomfortable, we can always sit in a natural cross-legged posture (*sukhāsana*), although in such a posture the knees point higher into the air, increasing the stress on our lower back. Moreover, in a normal cross-legged position our ankle bones tend to press against each other, causing an additional discomfort that does not occur in half-lotus (where the ankles are kept far away from one another). For this reason half-lotus is highly recommended, and if we have to perform exercises to stretch our hip flexor muscles, such an effort is well worth it.

Woolen Āsana

Another essential object for our meditation practice is a woolen yoga *āsana* (seat). Traditionally, the woolen *āsana* is a thin woolen square that is placed over our meditation cushion. Although our rug already performs the task of insulating us from the floor beneath, adding a woolen *āsana* fulfills two additional functions. The first is that by sitting on the same cloth over and over again, our *āsana* accumulates a little of the Shakti that is drawn down during meditation, so when we sit for our next session, the vibrations in the *āsana* enable us to meditate with less effort. Second, our seat is a symbol of the power and presence of the inner Guru. When we sit on an *āsana*, we surrender our body and mind to the Guru and we honor our own divinity; just as a king's throne represents the power of the office of the king, in the same way the yogin's *āsana* represents the power of yoga that flows directly from God. In this way our *āsana* serves as an elegant symbol that reminds us of the immense opportunity and privilege of being able to meditate.

Duration

One of the most common questions is, "For how long should I meditate?" Some teachers suggest sitting for twenty minutes or half an hour, or setting aside time for two sessions a day, one at dawn and the other at dusk. Others recommend meditating only for as long as the session lasts, meaning until we experience a natural break in our concentration or absorption.

Personally, I recommend making a strong mental commitment to sit for a full hour. This is because in the beginning most of our meditation hour will be spent lost in a cauldron of thoughts, and until we build up some strength of mind, we will only be able to experience a true quieting of our thoughts near the end of our session, perhaps for a period lasting three to five minutes at most. For this reason, if we want to have any hope of experiencing deeper states of consciousness, we need to move beyond the mindset that we are sitting to enjoy a little relaxation for a short period of time. The purpose of meditation, of course, is to become aware of our own I-consciousness, and to stabilize in that experience. Ultimately, we should aim to sit for one and a half hours, but we can spend many years meditating for our hour with great results. Beyond the one-hour mark, the force of our meditation is what carries us through.

The ability to sit for one hour is easier than it might at first seem. It is simply a question of making a firm resolve. To track time, we can have a digital clock plugged into the wall opposite to where we sit or we can program a bell to ring at the end of one hour. If we use a clock, we must be sure to note the exact time when we first sit, and if our eyes happen to open too soon, we should simply close them again and resume our practice. By never rising before our allotted time, our mind will learn how to stay focused for longer periods until meditating for a full hour feels perfectly natural.

If, for whatever reason, we find it impossible to sit for a full hour, we can gradually build up to a complete hour over the initial months of practice.

Approaching Our Meditation Seat

So we have woken up before dawn, taken a shower, and had a few sips of water. We have also dressed in our meditation clothes. Now, as we approach our meditation seat, we must bring awareness to the act. Approaching our seat is not the same as plopping ourselves down on our sofa. Instead, we should approach with a feeling of offering. What is it exactly that we are offering? We are offering our mind and body into the fire of yoga.

When we approach our seat, we should do so with a feeling of humility and reverence. If we have a physical Guru, we can take a moment to light a candle or oil lamp before his or her picture. Then we should kneel before our seat and bow fully, allowing our forehead to touch the edge of our *āsana*. The act of bowing is more than just symbolic. When we bow, our heart chakra is lifted higher than our head. It signifies that our heart (consciousness) is above our mind (intellect). Bowing is an act of deep reverence. It enhances humility and devotion. Bowing, in fact, is how we acknowledge our love for our own inner Self. It is a prelude to surrender, which naturally unfolds as our practice deepens and matures.

Taking Our Seat

After bowing, we finally settle down on our meditation seat, folding our legs into half-lotus posture. If we are so inclined, we can join our palms together in *anjali mudrā* (salutation seal). Next we should place our hands on our knees, palms down, in *chin mudrā*. (I prefer to have my hands palm down, while others like to meditate with their palms up in *jñāna mudrā*.) Either way is fine, although in *chin mudrā* the wrists are not rotated. As mentioned above, *chin mudrā* is important because when our thumbs form a circle with our forefingers, it recirculates our energy, increasing our vibrational frequency.

At this point our posture should feel steady and grounded, and our knees should be resting comfortably on the floor. There should be no strain on our lower back or pain in our legs. Next, we can lift our chin and roll our shoulders a couple of times to help straighten our back. This is where using a proper meditation cushion really pays off, as it allows us to maintain a straight back effortlessly. If we were sitting directly on the rug, our lower back would hunch after only a few minutes. And if we still detect any strain on our lower back, it means our cushion is too low. Likewise, if we feel we might fall out of balance at any moment, then our cushion is too high.

Preliminary Practices: *Dhāraṇās* to Help Center the Mind

Now we close our eyes, checking that our back is as straight as an arrow. Our neck is soft, without tension, and our jaw equally relaxed. Our mouth is closed, with the tip of our tongue resting on the upper palate just behind our front teeth.

We take a few long and deep breaths. In meditation we always breathe through the nose, and at a natural pace. We are not yet trying to meditate, but only focusing on gently opening our lungs in order to establish a good flow of oxygen. We inhale deep and exhale long for five or six rotations, until we feel that our lungs are nice and open. Then we allow our breathing to gently return to its normal rhythm.

Turning toward the mind, we become aware of just how

restless the thought stream really is. It feels as though the moment we try to quiet the mind, it rebels by kicking up a storm of thoughts.

Luckily, the mind's behavior is both natural and to be expected, so the first lesson is that the upsurge in thoughts is no cause for concern. We *can* meditate and our efforts are not doomed to fail. Worries about failure play directly into the ego's strategy of self-preservation, and even though our mind has been humbly cooperating until this point, it still remains a thief dressed up as a policeman pretending to be a devotee.

Since our mind is not going to cooperate until the Shakti takes hold of it, we should simply take note of our agitated mind and practice any of the *dhāraṇās* (contemplations and visualizations) below which are designed to calm our thoughts and invoke the Guru's grace.[61] It bears repeating, however, that the *dhāraṇās* stand apart from the core practice of meditation, which means we must let go of them as soon as they have fulfilled their purpose. In addition, each *dhāraṇā* should not consume more than three or four minutes of our time.

First Dhāraṇā: Breathing In Light, Breathing Out Thoughts

Maintaining closed eyes, we bring our attention back to our breath. Inhaling slowly and deeply, we visualize streams of white light entering our being, and as we breathe out, we visualize streams of grey or black smoke (representing our agitated thoughts) leaving our body. As we repeat the exercise, the grey smoke gradually turns white, until the last traces of restlessness have been removed from our system. We can repeat the exercise for as many cycles as needed until the grey smoke has turned completely white. After our breath returns

---

61. Here the word *dhāraṇā* is not used with the same meaning as found in the sixth limb of Patañjali's *Yoga Sūtra*, where it is defined as the repeated effort to maintain attention on a single object of perception. In our context it means a contemplation or visualization exercise.

to normal, we rest for a few moments in the radiance of the white light that surrounds us both from within and without.

Second Dhāraṇā: Guru Mānasa Pūjā, or Mental Worship of the Guru

If we are devoted to a particular Guru, we can spend a minute or two mentally worshipping the Guru after invoking his or her image. We can visualize the majestic form of Sri Guru sitting peacefully or we can go a step further and perform simple rituals such as offering flowers and fruit at his feet, draping him in a beautiful woolen shawl, garlanding him, or even visualizing the steps of a *pāda pūjā* (adoration of the feet) whereby milk, coconut water, and honey are poured over the feet, which are then rinsed and adorned with marks of sandalwood paste and white ash.

In whatever way we wish to worship our Guru, the act of holding the image of an authentically Self-realized being in our mind is one of the sweetest and most powerful practices available to a devotee. I find that when I hold Sri Bhagawan's image in my mind, a deep stillness and devotional mood quickly envelop my being, and the rolling thought waves naturally begin to settle down.

Third Dhāraṇā: Nyāsa, Installing the Guru and Mantra in Our Body

Keeping our beloved Guru's form in mind, we can move on to the blissful practice of *nyāsa* (placing the Guru in the body). If we have received a mantra, we can begin to silently repeat it, harmonizing one repetition per breath (even better is to start repeating our mantra the moment we rise from bed). We bring our attention into our *mūlādhāra* chakra and visualize our Guru sitting at its center. We breathe into the chakra once or twice before moving up to the next chakra until we reach the *sahasrāra* (thousand-petal lotus) above the head, all the while repeating our mantra. Next we install our Guru in our eyes, ears, mouth, hands, and feet, after which we return our attention to the *sahasrāra* and visualize our Guru sitting peacefully at the center of the lotus, his skin shining like the full moon, his countenance radiating unspeakable power and grace.

Holding the image of the Guru in the *sahasrāra* is a sacred practice in and of itself since it causes the *prāna* in the body to rise upward, instantly quieting the mind and reducing identification to the body. It allows us to connect to the grace-bestowing power of the Guru and draws down Shakti in a powerful way.

The simple practice of installing the Guru is, in my experience, beautiful beyond measure. When I honor Bhagawan Nityananda by installing him through *nyāsa*, I feel that I am benefiting from his direct protection and grace. I find that the vibration of my mantra intensifies many times over when I join it to his image. By installing Sri Bhagawan in both body and mind, I practice becoming one with him, and there is nothing more joyful for a devotee. This is one of the reasons why I feel so much enthusiasm to get up each dawn and meditate, because I know that I will be able to spend a few minutes merging with my Guru.

After sitting quietly in this way, we can envision that our body has been completely replaced with that of our Guru, holding onto the feeling for a few minutes. Alternatively, after visualizing our Guru sitting in front of us, we should try to experience that the awareness behind his or her eyes is the same, identical awareness behind our eyes (in the same way that when we look into a mirror we correlate the awareness behind the eyes in the reflection to our own awareness). By joining the awareness behind two different bodies, we complete an initial step in the process of identification, surrender, and absorption.

As the reader may have noticed, up to this point the contemplations are external in nature insofar as they invoke the Guru's physical presence, which is particularly helpful when the mind is in an externalized and turbulent state.

At this stage we should be no more than five to seven minutes into our session, and from here on, the *dhāraṇās* that follow will more directly target our innate I-consciousness.

Fourth Dhāraṇā: Using the Breath as a Centering Device

While not a *dhāraṇā* in the strict sense of the word (because imagination and visualization are not used), using our breath as a device to make contact with pure Awareness is a core technique which we will return to again and again. While it properly belongs to the central practice of meditation, I am introducing it here since the final *dhāraṇās* listed below yield better results when we first take a moment to center our mind.

After letting go of our Guru's image, we breathe in slowly, tracing our inhalation to its source. We hold our breath for one or two seconds before releasing, allowing the brief pause to bring our I-consciousness to the center of our attention.

Since the space between each breath or between each thought is where pure Consciousness resides (and because both breath and thought rise up from the same source), gently arresting the breath induces a natural pause in our thoughts, allowing pure Awareness to more easily shine through. And while it is not necessary to always pause the breath in order to locate Awareness, doing so at first is helpful until we have become familiar with our I-feeling. After our breathing returns to normal we should strive to keep our attention locked onto our I-feeling despite the resumption of thoughts.

We can repeat this centering technique three or four times until we feel more anchored in the empty awareness between each breath.[62]

It bears mentioning that holding the breath for a second or two does not amount to the practice of *prāṇāyāma* (breath control). Both the brevity of the pause and of the entire *dhāraṇā* do not equate with the strenuous and forceful

---

62. We can adopt this practice at any point in the day when we feel our mind grow restless.

exercises that some paths advocate as a means to still the mind. On the contrary, in our approach, the mind is never wrestled into submission, but is instead allowed to quiet down naturally as a result of proper technique.

Fifth Dhāraṇā: Eliminating the Universe in One Fell Swoop

Before we begin to meditate in earnest, there a few more *dhāraṇās* that can be done very quickly—in a matter of seconds —which can further help us solidify our contact with the Self.

With a calm mind, we imagine that all of creation, the entire universe in fact, is suddenly wiped out of existence. What remains? Only pure Awareness remains, the formless feeling that we exist, and we rest in the feeling of being that Awareness.

As mentioned above, this contemplation works best when done quickly. This *dhāraṇā* is not about identifying and negating things one layer at a time, as in the *neti, neti* practice. Here, our thoughts, our body, the room we are sitting in, and the greater world outside—all of it is to be dissolved instantly, so that nothing but pure Awareness remains, revealing to us that the feeling that we exist persists even in the absence of all objectivity.

Sixth Dhāraṇā: Stepping Outside the Flow of Time

Instead of focusing on the dissolution of space, we can choose to focus on the dissolution of time.

Sitting quietly, we can imagine that absolutely all movement in the universe has ceased. Everything has ground to a halt, even down to the movement of molecules and atoms. Once everything has grown still, we should contemplate whether it is still possible to tell time. The answer, of course, is that time can no longer be measured since time is nothing but a measure of change. Time, in other words, is only a measure of surface change, like movie images dancing on a white screen that never moves, and if all motion is suddenly arrested, then only the eternal present will be felt to exist. The

82

shift from flowing through time to feeling the stillness of the present moment is similar to the shift our eyes make from looking through a glass to seeing our own reflection. When we step back, as it were, into our I-feeling, we become aware of a "place" where neither movement nor change are possible.

Contemplating in this way allows us to literally step out of time as we shift our identity from the moving objects that make up creation to the perfect stillness that is found when we locate our I-feeling. With a little practice, in an instant this *dhāraṇā* can move us powerfully into an awareness of pure Being.

Seventh Dhāraṇā: Recognizing Thoughts as Flowing Streams of Consciousness

A final *dhāraṇā* worth considering is particularly useful when, despite our best efforts, our thoughts refuse to stop racing, holding our attention hostage. In order to neutralize them we can try viewing our thoughts not as thoughts per se, but as flowing streams of consciousness. The *Shiva Sūtras* states *cittaṁ mantraḥ*,[63] mind is mantra, and when we recognize the energy propelling our thoughts as well as the thoughts themselves as nothing but consciousness coalesced into vibrations of sound, we will find that they naturally dissolve into stillness. When we view thoughts as consciousness, we neither grasp nor reject them, which allows us to move past them.

When the mind is particularly rebellious, we can resist the impulse to try stopping it by force. Instead, we can simply observe the flow of images, thoughts, and memories, knowing that they are but streams of consciousness and that the Presence which is aware of them also happens to be their source. Remembering that, as a knowing subject, we must be present before we can even claim to be disturbed by something naturally draws our attention back to our own awareness. This Tantric practice differs from common forms of *vipassanā* in

63. *Shiva Sūtras* 2:1.

83

that by recognizing thoughts as consciousness, we subsume thoughts into consciousness, as opposed to simply watching them as objects from afar.

It is helpful to keep in mind that engaging in any of the above *dhāraṇās* is entirely optional. Although on principle I always perform the worship and installation of my Guru, I only rely on other contemplations when I feel the need to. If in the beginning the *dhāraṇās* feel artificial or simply like exercises in imagination, then after breathing deeply and opening our lungs, we can move directly into our main practice. As our contact with the Self deepens over time, the *dhāraṇās* will grow more useful in helping us locate the ground of Awareness.

The Essence of Meditation

Up to this point, we have been sitting quietly on our yoga *āsana* in a comfortable posture, holding our spine erect. Our breathing is natural and we feel relaxed. To help clear the initial rush of thoughts, we may have availed ourselves of any of the *dhāraṇās* mentioned above. Now, with closed eyes, we can finally dive into the heart of our meditation practice.

As mentioned earlier, the skillful use of a mantra offers a highly accessible entry point into true meditative absorption, more so in my experience than many other well-known methods. Accordingly, we will practice a meditation technique that is centered on a mantra, subdividing it into two different phases: the first, using mantra as a direct method of attainment, and the second, relegating mantra to a supporting role. While both approaches can stand on their own, it often follows that as our mind grows one-pointed, the first method naturally gives way to the second, which is why I define them as phases.

The question can still be asked: Of all possible techniques, why mantra? Why not focus directly on our I-feeling which we have identified as the most direct method of attainment?

As already pointed out, doing so for sustained periods of time might prove difficult unless we are highly practiced. Instead, we can train up to pure Self-attention by first practicing with an authentic mantra since it offers a powerful and proven route into the formless Self. In addition to being a well of auspiciousness, holy mantras are safe, offer a strong aura of protection, and can be grasped by aspirants both of untrained or subtle mind (the more subtle the mind, the more the mantra will reveal itself as pure Consciousness). Moreover, for readers who are not in relationship with a particular Guru or who have not been initiated into a particular lineage, mantra practiced with heartfelt devotion offers immediate and universal access to the Guru's Shakti.

As a matter of fact, page after page can be dedicated to singing the glories of mantra, but what is most needed is the understanding that mantra is the very sound form of the Lord and that repeating it with proper awareness and technique can lead us to full Self-realization. Eventually, if we succeed in uniting with our mantra, we reach a point where the articulated mantra gives way to the vibrating silence of pure Awareness, and in that moment we are able to cognize that the mantra, the witness of the mantra, and the pure Consciousness we call God have always been one and the same, which leads directly into pure Self-attention.

Phase I: Uniting with a Sacred Mantra

The first phase in meditating with a mantra entails learning how to properly unite with it. As mentioned, the key is to avoid repeating it in a mechanical way. To elaborate, a distinction can be made between proper and improper absorption into an object of concentration. If we concentrate deeply on an object of perception, such as a mantra or a *yantra*, the resultant union may terminate in a temporary and stupefying abeyance of the mind that does not lead into Self-awareness. We risk this outcome when we view our object of focus as a mere object that is separate from us. For example, if we experience our mantra as just a string of ordinary letters and words, we may eventually succeed in fusing with it, but we will only experience a stupor-like suppression of the mind. On the other hand, if we consciously repeat our mantra with the awareness that it is a manifest expression of our own innate consciousness, then union with the mantra will lead us directly into authentic Self-awareness.

We start by silently repeating our mantra (if we have not been initiated into a mantra, we can choose to repeat the supremely auspicious and grace bestowing *Om Namaḥ Shivāya*), synchronizing one repetition to the inbreath and one to the outbreath. We allow ourselves to grow comfortable with the gentle ebb and flow of the mantra, becoming aware not only of the sound of the gross syllables but of their inherent vibration of energy.

If we are new to the mantra, it might take several weeks to truly get used to it, and we will not be able to make much progress beyond simply listening to the mantra as we repeat it. If this is our situation, then our only work at this stage is to gently bring the mind back to the mantra as soon as we realize our attention has drifted away. This simple practice is in and of itself highly purifying, and it is an important and noble first step in our journey toward *samādhi*.

After a few weeks or even a few months of practice, we can begin in earnest the process of uniting with the mantra. As just described, we must overcome the feeling that we are a person repeating a mantra. Instead, we must strive diligently to unite the mantra to our I-consciousness, so that our knowing subject, the mantra itself, and its meaning all merge into a unified pulsation of Awareness.

To accomplish this, we must make efforts to listen intently to the mantra as we repeat it, making sure to bring our attention right back to it the moment another thought distracts us. After giving the mantra our full attention, we can tell ourselves that there is no actual person or entity who is repeating the mantra, but that the sound of *Om Namaḥ Shivāya* is effectively repeating itself. After practicing like this for some time, we should then try to experience that the awareness that is witnessing the mantra has become the sounds of the mantra itself. These two movements of mind are what enable our I-feeling to unite with the mantra.

If at any point our attention shifts out to our body, our breath, or the room we are sitting in, we can tell ourselves that these things are not separate objects but that they are composed of the vibration of the mantra. Then we should quickly return our attention to the sound of the mantra, trying our best to once again fuse our sense of being and the mantra into a single awareness. In other words, after locating the consciousness that is witnessing the mantra, we extend or project that presence directly into the mantra, which in time will allow us to experience that the mantra is nothing other than pure Consciousness and that the mantra is all that exists.

We should sit with this practice for as long as we need to, until the mere thought of union gives way to the actual feeling that there is no separation between the mantra and the witness of the mantra. In fact, many meditators spend years with this single practice, and it alone can result in full meditative absorption. Once union with the mantra is achieved, which is a gradual process that cannot be rushed or forced, the mantra itself disappears, plunging the mind into deeper states of consciousness.

If we persist in replacing or uniting our sense of being with that of the mantra, after a few months we will notice (usually only during the final few minutes of our session) a shift in awareness, where it truly feels that there is nothing other than the pulsation of *Om Namaḥ Shivāya*. We arrive at the experience that nothing outside of *Om Namaḥ Shivāya* exists, and in this way we might say that we allow ourselves to be consumed by the mantra. As our sense of body and mind begin to dissolve into the mantra, we notice that there is no longer any space for other thoughts to exist, and since the mantra is composed of divine vibrations that are naturally inward facing, we discover that the mantra begins to grow more and more subtle as the months go by.

While initially the mantra may only resonate in our mouth (sometimes the tongue tries to silently articulate the mantra as we repeat it, even though our mouth is closed), there comes a time when we experience the gross syllables being replaced by a more subtle and steady vibrational hum, and the mantra feels as if it has slipped down into our throat. Sometimes, instead of keeping to the rhythm of one repetition per breath, the mantra suddenly speeds up, so that it repeats itself three or four times with each breath. When this happens, the mantra fuses into something entirely different. It no longer remains as a clearly articulated *Om Namaḥ Shivāya* but transforms into a subtle murmur that vibrates intensely and charges the entire body with energy, indicating that the mantra's power is rising.

When the mantra behaves in this way, it indicates that the physical body has been sufficiently purified and that the mantra is now ready to work at the *mādhyama* or middling level of speech that corresponds to our subtle body.[64] When this happens, the energetic vibration of the mantra becomes even more intense, and in my own case the descent of the mantra into the throat marked the moment I was able to pierce the sleep barrier and enter into the first stage of *tandrā* (a subtle and highly visual state of consciousness that arises when one is able to penetrate into the point between the waking and sleep states. See chapter seven for a full discussion).

As our practice deepens, the mantra will eventually drop

---

64. The four levels of speech are *vaikharī* or gross, corresponding to the physical body; *mādhyama*, or subtle, corresponding to the subtle body; *paśyantī*, or causal, corresponding to the causal body; and *para*, or supreme, corresponding to the transcendental state of consciousness.

into the heart chakra and finally into the navel chakra, with each progressive level of subtleness manifesting different kinds of spiritual experiences in accordance to our needs. But even in the earlier stages, there are moments when the mantra becomes so subtle that it suddenly disappears, allowing us to be absorbed for a few minutes in a perfect stillness where nothing is felt to exist other than an empty expanse of blissful Awareness.

Some teachers claim that *Om Namaḥ Shivāya* is a beginner mantra that cannot take us to full enlightenment. Others say that for it to emit power it has to be repeated with a nasal upturn. All this is to be ignored, because in reality the initial gross repetitions of all mantras have little or no power. Power unfolds as the mantra becomes subtle through proper and sustained repetition, i.e., we invest it with Awareness. In time, mantras yield bliss and peace, as well as initiating all yogic processes. In fact, when the mantra moves into a state of dynamic stillness, the natural unstruck sounds known as *nāda* begin to manifest.[65] Sometimes, new and unknown mantras spontaneously arise out of the vibrating stillness, and the mind automatically repeats them with tremendous results.

For these reasons, mantra repetition, when done properly, offers a reliable and extremely enjoyable path to reach the Self that for some may prove a little easier to practice than direct Self-attention. When we are successful in uniting the mantra to our sense of being, after some time the mantra will dissolve, which signals its fulfillment, leaving us absorbed in profound stillness. In this way, even though the mantra begins as a secondary object of perception, proper union with it makes it capable of leading us right back into the pure Self.

---

65. Different scriptures name ten divine inner sounds that are heard when the *prāna* enters the central channel or penetrates into the *sahasrāra*. They include bells, chimes, conch, thunder, clapping, flute, buzzing of bees, and so on.

Phase II: Using the Mantra as Rails to Guide Us Into Self-Awareness

While uniting with the mantra is an excellent method of practice, a second approach, which may be considered more advanced, entails not focusing on the vibration of the mantra per se, but holding our attention firm in the empty I-feeling between each repetition (which also happens to be the space between each breath, since the mantra and the breath are for the most part synchronized).

In reality, I do not consider moving from the sound of the mantra to the silence in the middle as a separate practice, but as a natural progression of the first. That is, after uniting strongly with the mantra over a period of months or years, we will discover that after a few minutes of repetition our attention naturally gravitates toward our I-consciousness, which is both its source as well as the seat of pure Awareness. In this approach, we do not so much merge into mantra as use it as rails to guide us directly into our I-consciousness.

As we sit, we relax deeply into our innate I-feeling that is found between each mantra repetition and between each breath. Here we do not pay overt attention to our mantra; rather the mantra performs the dual function of keeping other thoughts at bay and of providing a framework for locating our Self. It is as if the mantra acts like the trail of blue lights that illumines each side of an airport runway.

As we repeat the mantra, our attention does not move with the sound but remains fixed at the center. If our attention gets dragged into the mantra or into any other thought or perception, we gently bring it back to the pure Awareness that is observing the mantra in the first place.

Fixing our attention in the space between each repetition is only the first step. Next we must strive to unite with our I-consciousness, feeling that we are that empty space and that the mantra, the breath, our body, and everything else both emanates and is contained within that pure center of consciousness.

As we settle more deeply into the stillness between each repetition, we will find that everything begins to melt or dissolve into that empty space, including the feeling that we are watching it, so that in the end only pure Awareness rests in pure Awareness. Even the mantra gives way to pure silence, and we reach a point where only stillness is aware of stillness, meaning that there is no longer any awareness of being a body.

In practice, we should guard against having any kind of expectations or judgments, for these are nothing but thoughts that shift attention away from the Self. Instead, we try to drop all thoughts as they arise, doing our best to rest quietly in our pure I-feeling. Even the idea that we are struggling to become established in pure Awareness is a thought to let go of. Likewise, there is no point in wondering when we are going to break through into the next stage of practice, or whether we are making any progress. All of these thoughts are nothing but disruptions that take us away from settling deeply into the Awareness that we already are and have always been.

Taking the support of a mantra allows us to come full circle to Sadhu Om's practice of Self-attention, since the silence at the center of each repetition is none other than the I-feeling Sadhu Om instructs us to focus on. But instead of practicing in the midst of a sea of ordinary thoughts, which are outward facing and object oriented, framing our attention in the space between repetitions of *Om Namaḥ Shivāya* lessens the chance that our mind will be dragged away into an endless stream of random thoughts.

Real penetration into our I-feeling will only occur when our attention is able to rest in itself or, put differently, when our awareness becomes aware of itself. To clear the mind, we take the help of a mantra, first working with its gross sound and refining our understanding until we are able to completely unite with it, moving thereafter into the heart of awareness which lies at the center of each repetition. Once we are able to successfully settle into the stillness between the mantra repetitions, we have reached the dawn of true meditation absorption, and from then it is only a matter of time before we are able to pierce the sleep barrier, penetrating into the inner landscapes of *tandrā* that precede the lightning rise of the Kundalini Shakti.

Yet, prior to gaining the strength to penetrate into *tandrā*, we will spend many hours absorbed in an intensely blissful and thoughtless awareness that feels electrically charged, which might give us the false sense that we have reached the "end of the road." Instead, we should understand that settling into our I-feeling does not in the least amount to final liberation, which only transpires after the Kundalini rises and the subtle process of *krama mudrā* is complete (see chapter seven). As discussed earlier, our I-feeling is still a form of ego that is filled with mental impressions called *saṃskāras* or *vāsanas* that need to be transcended.

In other words, penetrating into the formless awareness at the center of the mind is only a prelude to *tandrā*. It is therefore very important to keep meditating with a "continually refreshed awareness," as Swami Lakshmanjoo teaches, meaning that our concentration, alertness, and awareness remain unbroken at all times.[66]

While moving from emptiness into *tandrā* might seem counterintuitive (since it seems strange that after reaching a state of deep bliss and stillness we should suddenly revert back into a world of vivid perceptions), it is quite understandable when viewed from the perspective of purifying the mind from its storehouse of latent impressions.

In addition, even though passage through some expression

66. John Hughes, *Self Realization in Kashmir Shaivism: The Oral Teachings of Swami Lakshmanjoo* (Albany: State University of New York Press, 1995).

of *tandrā* is unavoidable for the vast majority of us, like all other observable phenomena, *tandrā* is a temporary state which will eventually pass. Without grasping or rejecting anything that appears in *tandrā*, we should keep our attention turned inward so as not to deviate from the core practice of awareness resting in awareness, which is the one true action that leads to permanent Self-awareness.

A final observation is that there is no set timeline for moving from the sound of the mantra to focusing directly on our I-feeling between each repetition. As mentioned earlier, some yogins practice uniting with the vibration of mantra for their entire lives. Others, from the start, focus their attention on the I-consciousness found between each repetition, while a third group of meditators migrate from sound to I-feeling in their own time. Whatever our approach, as long as we practice *japa* correctly, i.e., with proper awareness, the mantra will eventually bring us into the state of *tandrā*.

Meditating without the Support of a Mantra

What happens if for some reason we resist the idea of re-peating a Sanskrit mantra altogether? Because of religious affiliation or simply because Sanskrit mantras seem too long, too difficult, or too foreign to pronounce, some people have trouble with the idea of repeating a mantra. In such cases two options present themselves: The first is to follow the practices described above by reducing *Om Namaḥ Shivāya* to *Om*. The monosyllable *Om*, of course, is short and easy to synchronize to the breath, although for some people even *Om* many not resolve issues of religious affiliation. In such cases a second option is to employ the natural flow of the breath as a substitute for the mantra.

If we listen carefully, we will notice that both the ingoing and outgoing breaths carry their own subtle sound. Both the scriptures and sages have brought that sound to the forefront by suggesting that we hear *so* on the inbreath and *ham* (heard

93

as hum) on the outbreath. Alternatively, the Shaivite tradition suggests *ham* on the inbreath and *sa* on the outbreath.[67] But while *So'ham* repetition is a powerful practice, a sound like this that is so deeply commingled with the flow of the breath carries the risk of being too subtle for the beginner's mind to stick with throughout a full hour of meditation. The subtlety of the sound might allow our attention to slip back into the thought stream or, after a while, we might simply drift into sleep.

Nevertheless, I am not suggesting that meditation on *So'ham* should not be attempted. If a strong effort is made to stay alert and centered, *So'ham* may prove to be the only practice we ever need. Alternatively, we can dispense with all types of breath and sound supports and focus directly on our I-feeling, just as Sri Ramana instructed.

With these options, there is no reason (cultural, religious, or otherwise) to believe we cannot direct our attention into our I-feeling. But it is also important to reiterate that none of these efforts will matter if our heart is not brimming with enthusiasm to practice. As the saying goes, *bhāva* (feeling) is everything, and it is here that devotion to a Guru is so helpful because it allows us to associate our love of Self-awareness with a form. Without *bhakti*, or devotion, we will find it difficult to sustain a daily practice during periods when our mind is particularly rebellious or uncooperative, or when we face serious challenges in our lives.

Without a deep love of meditation fueling our efforts through all the highs and lows, it will be almost impossible to make significant progress. Yet, we should not feel discouraged. Devotion is also the fruit of practice, and since practice is necessary whether we have devotion or not, we can move forward with confidence, trusting that our sincere efforts will one day transform our heart into an ocean of love.

67. *So'ham* is mentioned, among other places, in the *Yoga Shikha Upanishad*. *Hamsa* was favored by the great eleventh-century master Kshemaraja.

Where to Focus Our Mind

Whether we are meditating on the mantra or directly on our I-feeling, a common question concerns whether we should simultaneously rest our attention within any particular chakra. In other words, even though our attention may be on the words of the mantra, it is also possible to place that mantra within any of the seven chakras. Traditionally, the recommendation has been to focus our attention either on the heart center, the *ājñā* chakra in between the eyebrows, or in the space just above the crown of our head. Indeed, at the start of our session, we might find it helpful to pool our attention into the *ājñā* chakra for a few seconds before moving into the preliminary *dhāraṇās* discussed earlier. The *ājñā* chakra is a command center which is also the seat of the supreme *praṇava*, the vibration of Om, and resting there naturally elevates our *prāna*.

As we meditate, we progressively draw down Shakti which triggers a diversity of purificatory *kriyās*, and we might find that from time to time our attention is pulled into one or another chakra, facilitating the divine energy's work in that plexus. When this happens, it is best to allow our attention to rest wherever the Shakti is drawing it until we experience a natural release from that space. Then we should return to union with the mantra and/or absorption into our I-feeling.

As a general rule, it is not necessary to make a conscious decision to limit attention to any particular chakra given that both the mantra and our I-feeling are all-pervading. In fact, Sri Ramana spoke against it. When asked if our attention should be placed at the center between the eyebrows, he said:

> The feeling "I Am" is directly evident to everyone. What happiness is there in seeing any particular God if one ignores this feeling? There is no foolishness like that of thinking that God exists only in certain spots such as the place between the eyebrows. Fixing the attention on these spots is just a violent form of *sādhanā* whose aim

is to concentrate the mind in order to prevent it from running everywhere. Enquiring "Who am I?" (i.e., resting on our I-feeling) is a much easier method of controlling the mind.[68]

Emerging from Meditation

As our concentration begins to wane near the end of our session, we will find that our awareness becomes extroverted and that the energies in our body slowly return to normal. If we open our eyes and notice we are short of our one-hour target, we should close them again and gently bring our attention back to the mantra, regardless of how active our mind feels. This kind of discipline is similar to pushing a muscle during a workout, and in time the mind will be trained to remain interiorized for the full hour.

After opening our eyes, we can take a few deep breaths and continue to sit quietly for a few minutes, basking in the energy around us. We should never rush out of meditation, for how we come out affects how we come into our next session. When we are ready, we can join our hands in *añjali mudrā*, thanking God for giving us the opportunity to meditate.

As we move our legs, we might feel a sharp pain in our ankles or in some other part. Sitting for an hour can cause our legs to hurt, and a neat trick is to put pressure on an aching ankle by pressing our calf over it or by lifting ourselves from our *āsana* and sitting in *vajrāsana*, facing our meditation seat. If we let all the weight of our body rest on our ankles, the pain will dissipate quickly. We can end our session by bowing down to our yoga *āsana* once again, visualizing our beloved Guru or another form of God before us.

Once done, we should change out of our meditation clothes so as to avoid walking around the house in them. As mentioned earlier, as we meditate, our clothes as well as

68. Sri Ramana quoted in Godman, *Living By the Words of Bhagavan*.

our *āsana* accumulate Shakti, which helps to ease us into our next session.

Bringing Our Meditation into the World

While our formal hour of meditation forms the core of our *sādhanā*, the rest of our day presents an opportunity for us to practice awareness by returning our attention to our I-feeling as often as possible.

When we meditate, we are able to still our minds in powerful ways, and the mental impressions left behind after we emerge from our session can be harnessed to further our practice even as we go about our day. In other words, focusing our attention on our I-consciousness is much more effective when supported by a formal meditation practice, and likewise, the more we practice awareness during our waking state, the deeper our meditation sessions will become.

If we are not focusing directly on our I-feeling, we can also choose to repeat our mantra as often as possible (not forgetting to unite our identity to the mantra as discussed earlier) or better yet, repeat the mantra while keeping our attention on the motionless awareness between each repetition. In this way, we are able to carry our formal practice into our day, which raises the question whether there is any real difference between them.

The answer is an unequivocal "yes!" I cannot stress enough that while practicing awareness during our normal waking state is extremely important, in my experience there is no substitute for formal meditation, since it is only then that we will be able to still our mind and equalize the breath in a way that is simply not going to occur while practicing throughout the day. The intense rise of Shakti and the utter bliss, peace, and stillness experienced in meditation are very difficult to attain while our mind is flowing out like a river through our five senses.

At times, if we experience difficulty becoming aware of

awareness, we can practice a quick *dhāraṇā* that works well when our body is in motion. In this contemplation, we attempt to experience that we are not moving within space, but that we are *behind* space watching it flow by—like standing at the bank of a river watching the rushing waters go by.

When, for example, we are walking down the street, after locating our sense of being, we can immediately try to feel that our consciousness is not moving. That is, our body and the things around us are certainly moving, but we, the knowing subject, are perfectly still even as our body advances down the street.

If we think about a person staring into a kaleidoscope, the person's eye does not move while the kaleidoscope turns and turns, displaying a variety of colorful patterns. In the same way, we can try to experience that while the world is in motion around us, we, the pure Consciousness, witness it in perfect stillness. This "walking-in-stillness" *dhāraṇā*, when practiced properly, is a powerful method to ground our attention back into our I-feeling and to make us aware that the entire universe exists within us.

In truth, unless we continue to practice awareness as we go about our day, our meditation will not be very strong. Meditation is not an isolated event that happens once a day, but is simply the most intense hour in what should be a continuous practice of Self-awareness.

Practicing awareness throughout the day feeds the fire of meditation, and when we sit down for our next session we will find that our mind sinks into stillness much more rapidly. Moreover, if we do not make efforts to hold our attention on our I-feeling, there is every probability that our formal practice will begin to feel mechanical and dry, or that our minds will be dragged back into worldly desires, making it very difficult to keep to our daily commitment.

CHAPTER SIX

Kriyās and Other Distractions

One of the issues meditators have to face, usually sooner than later, is how to handle movements, itches, discomfort, cramps, and so on during their meditation session.

Contrary to conventional wisdom, when something begins to itch, the best thing to do is to scratch it, allowing us to return quickly to our mantra repetition. If we try to be heroes and ignore the itch, we will waste most of our time thinking about the itch instead of our mantra. The same goes for aches. For example, if our ankle begins to hurt, we should shift our position slightly, the idea being to get comfortable as quickly as possible so we can return to our primary focus. Needless to say, if we are in constant pain or find ourselves constantly adjusting our position, then there is something off with our posture, our seat, or our body (here we are referring to minor itches or aches that surface once in a while and interfere with our meditation). As our absorption into the mantra or into our I-feeling grows stronger, we will be able to successfully ignore these kinds of distractions until they fade away of their own accord.

Some teachers suggest that once we start meditating, we should remain as still as a statue. Although it is good to remain as still as possible (and with a straight back), as the Shakti begins to accumulate and spread throughout our body, we might discover our body making spontaneous movements. These natural *kriyās* indicate that the Shakti is working to remove blockages at the physical and subtle levels. The removal of blockages allows the *prana* to flow properly throughout the body, preparing it to withstand the intense energy that comes with higher states of awareness. *Kriyās*, broadly applied, are not limited to physical movements but cover the range of all kinds of phenomena, including sensations, visions, sounds, emotions, thoughts, and illnesses that rise to the surface only to be expelled.

For example, in the early days sometimes my mouth would open for no reason (I mean open wide, like when we are sitting in the dentist's chair), and it remained open for several minutes at a time. At other times I would utter a sound, such as the syllable "Ha!," or a hissing sound might emerge out of nowhere. Sometimes my chin would point all the way up, stretching my neck, while at other times my chin went all the way down, touching the suprasternal notch at the base of the neck, placing me in *jalandhara bandha*. These physical locks, combined with certain spontaneous breathing patterns, would all occur naturally and without any thought or intention on my part. Yet at other times my upper body would spontaneously fold forward, so that my nose almost touched the carpet. As I continued to meditate, I went through a phase where my head would swing vigorously from side to side, as if gesturing an emphatic "no!" A few months later I experienced a deep, burning sensation in my left shoulder that would appear the moment I sat down and disappear the moment my session was over. This lasted for about a month. Later my hands and fingers began to arrange themselves into various *mudrās* or seals that are commonly seen in deity statues. For example, my hand would move into *abhaya mudrā* (the gesture of fearlessness) or *prāna mudrā* and hold for a few seconds before returning to *chin mudrā*. Sometimes my tongue would roll out of my mouth and stretch, as in the images of the Goddess Kali.

These are but a small sample of the hundreds of *kriyās* yogins might experience. *Kriyās* come and go on their own, and their variations are infinite. So when meditating, if we feel the sudden urge to move in a certain way, we should not resist. We should let our body react to the flow of energy while remaining a passive witness to the greatest extent possible, surrendering ourselves to the will of the supreme Shakti. Once the event has settled down, we can return to our core practice.

Not all *kriyās* occur while sitting in meditation. When I first started my *sādhanā*, I went through a period of highly intense *kriyās* and mystical experiences that preceded my *saṅkalpa dīkshā* by Sri Gurudev Bhagawan Nityananda. As I lay in bed, intense streams of heat would rush up and down my spine. While attending university lectures, I would feel a burning sensation over the *ājñā* chakra area, which was so strong it felt as if someone was pressing a red-hot penny between my eyebrows. Later, I began to experience extremely painful muscular contractions in the perineum area that were so sharp I actually went to visit a doctor. These contractions occurred many times a day, stopping me in my tracks (only later would I learn that the spasms indicated the movement of Shakti in or below the *mūlādhāra* chakra). At other times I experienced an intense pooling of energy in the *ājñā* chakra that created so much pressure that it radiated a terrible pain into my eye sockets.

Other *kriyās* that began to surface were mental in nature. As Shakti is drawn down during meditation, its reach extends deeply into our subconscious mind. Like a clear pool of water that becomes muddied when stirred with a stick, the Shakti causes many old and buried *samskāras* to rise to the surface. Unfortunately, the dislodging of old *samskāras* is usually not a pleasant experience, and sometimes they cause mental, emotional, or psychological symptoms as the dross is expunged from our system. In one instance, my mind was inundated with disturbing thoughts about a particular subject matter, and however hard I tried, I could not stop thinking about this particular thing. Then as suddenly as they had arrived, the clouds of thoughts lifted.

After these initial waves of purification, I began to have strong mystical experiences both in and out of formal meditation. I saw visions of various saints, some who would speak to me. The radiant pearl of blue light would stand before my sight, sometimes exploding into hundreds of scintillating blue dots. The blue light is particularly auspicious, as it is considered the visual form of the formless Self and was discussed extensively by Swami Muktananda.[69] Beyond the pearl, sometimes a blue flame about two inches in height would manifest before me, and when I opened my eyes, the blue flame would still be there, burning in the air in the middle of my room.

As I continued to meditate, I experienced a variety of other phenomena, such as the aura of white light mentioned earlier, or the lingering scent of roses after my meditation had ended. In dreams, I was visited by *siddhas* and gods, and experienced the auspicious omen of being bitten by a snake on my hand, on the back of my neck, and on my forehead.[70]

But what does it all mean? Should people press their palms together and bow their heads each time I walk into a room? Of course not. I share these precious gifts from the Guru only to highlight how an ordinary person like me, when armed with nothing but sincerity, devotion, and love of yoga, can initiate yogic processes in a short amount of time. All that is needed is a pure heart and a burning desire to merge into pure Awareness. As a matter of fact, while strong spiritual experiences are certainly encouraging, indicating that we are on the right path, they should not be taken as a mark of spiritual maturity or spiritual advancement. On the contrary, very strong spiritual phenomena can indicate that one is only at the beginner stages of *sādhanā*, since both *kriyās* and

69. See Swami Muktananda, *Play of Consciousness: A Spiritual Autobiography* (South Fallsburg, NY: SYDA Foundation, 1978).
70. When a yogin is bitten by a snake in dream, it signifies the blessings of the Kundalini Shakti.

mystical experiences diminish or disappear altogether after reaching higher levels of attainment. We must remember that *kriyās* are there to release blocks, purify and open pathways for the full descent of Shakti into the meditator, so it is common for a lot of activity to manifest as the Shakti first touches our network of energy channels. All kinds of pleasant and inspired visions can be experienced early on, as in my case, with deeper and horrifying kinds of visions (howling sounds, terrifying faces, apocalyptic scenes) sure to unfold once we reach a more advanced stage of absorption. (For those who are technically inclined, the negative images tend to arise just prior to the merging of the *prāna* and *apāna* into the *sushumnā nāḍī*.)

Moreover, what one yogin is destined to experience has nothing to do with the needs of the next person, so there is no template of *kriyās* to compare against. Some highly evolved meditators might pass into deep states of stillness without experiencing a single twitch or seeing a single light. Put simply, progress should never be measured by the presence or absence of *kriyās*, as we simply cannot foresee the kinds of purifications that are in store for us. *Kriyās* can remain active for a long time, only to disappear for months until they resurface unannounced. As our meditation deepens, the nature of our *kriyās* change. Only the divine Shakti knows what is in store for us.

For this reason, sages have cautioned us to ignore or simply observe in quiet reverence all phenomena that arises in meditation, or to view them as obstacles to be surmounted as quickly as possible. They become obstacles if we grow obsessed by them, hoping for repeat experiences. After all, as long as we are experiencing mystical phenomena, we are far away from the goal of pure meditative absorption, which is experienced as formless and devoid of all objects of perception, however sublime or inspired they may be. As long as there is a seer and a seen, we remain stuck in duality. The only thing we should be eager to experience is our perfect

I-consciousness along with the peace and bliss that are integral to its nature. Sri Nisargadatta Maharaj said the following:

> Looking outside for light and sound, all disciples undergo some spiritual experiences and that itself is bondage. They compare their experiences with others. Those disciples think they are very advanced. They are attracted to the experiences of sound and light, etc., because they identify themselves with the body. They want a shape and design; therefore, they revel in experiences which indicate shape and design.[71]

Consequently, those on Tantric yogic paths that focus attention on the awakening and movement of the Kundalini Shakti are vulnerable to becoming overly concerned with *kriyās* of all kinds, or with how much Shakti they have managed to draw down, or with how much Shakti they feel they have lost after indulging in sense pleasures of all kinds. Once the correct target of attention is lost, our progress grinds to a halt. One of the great advantages of the *jñāna-mārga*, the Vedantic path of knowledge, is that by placing all of one's focus directly on the pure I-feeling, the aspirant avoids over-scrutinizing the numerous yogic processes which are bound to unfold, instead merely acknowledging them as necessary but passing events. (It is a mistake to think that *jñāna* yogins do not experience or do not understand *kriyās* or Shakti.) After all, focusing on spiritual experiences does not beget spiritual experiences. Rather, focusing on ourselves as pure Awareness is what causes spiritual experiences to manifest in the first place.

In this light, while spiritual experiences should be cherished as a sign of the Guru's grace, they should be kept in perspective, lest they contaminate us with the worst kind of poison: spiritual pride. As long as we remain an individual

---

71. Jean Dunn, ed., *Consciousness and the Absolute: The Final Talks of Sri Nisargadatta Maharaj* (Durham, NC: Acorn Press, 1994).

who is capable of experiencing pride, we rest firmly in the jaws of delusion and spiritual ignorance. It is for this reason that we should never, ever elevate someone to the status of Guru simply because they are experiencing massive or "out of this world" spiritual fireworks. The true Guru is fully absorbed in his own Self and is beyond all experiences.

On a similar vein, the work the Shakti undertakes on our thoughts, emotions, and subconscious mind has caused some teachers to frame meditation and spiritual practice as if they are some kind of self-guided psychotherapy or psychoanalysis. There is much discussion on becoming aware of the deep layers of our mind, working with our emotional triggers, releasing mental blocks, and so forth. And while it is true that the Shakti coughs up all kinds of mental debris, we must remember that it is the Shakti that does all the work, not us, and that our only job is to either observe everything as a detached witness, or better, ignore everything so we can maintain our attention fixed on our I-consciousness.

While some meditators may not be able to detach from emotional *kriyās*, it is a mistake to intentionally try to be involved with any process the Shakti is unfolding, especially purifications that involve thought and emotion.[72] The Shakti, which is none other than the dynamic aspect of the Lord Himself, knows exactly how to purify our body and mind, and we should surrender fully to Her (the Shakti is always personified as a Goddess). If we are drawn into concepts of "working with the mind," we will only be adding fuel to the ego's fire, giving life to the limited personality we are trying to get rid of. Moreover, the attitude of trying to heal from negative emotions or other blocks can turn into a bottomless pit, and as mentioned above, our entire *sādhanā* risks becoming mired in waiting for *kriyās* to happen or in hoping to reach the

---

72. This is one of the reasons yogic traditions emphasize practicing within a community of meditators and under the expert guidance of a Guru or teacher.

next "level" of purification, for which there is no end in sight. In fact, obsessing over *kriyās* traps us in a victim mentality to the extent that we believe we are saddled with countless impurities. Instead of feeling pure and identifying with the light of supreme Consciousness, we end up identifying with the darkness of our mind, throwing us off the yogic path.

Although it may seem that there is no end to our thoughts or emotions, progress in yoga is like trying to saw through a thick tree branch on which we are sitting. For a long time we saw and saw, putting in all our effort until we can hardly lift an arm. And though it might feel as if we are making zero progress, in reality the saw cuts deeper and deeper into the branch, weakening it with each stroke of the blade. Then, unexpectedly, there comes a time when we and the entire branch come crashing down, marking a definite end to our struggles.

Sadhu Om puts it this way:

It takes a long time to prepare a temple cannon-blast, first putting the gunpowder into the barrel, giving the wick, adding some stones and then ramming it, but when ignited it explodes as a thunder in a split second. Similarly, after an age-long period of listening and reading (*śrāvaṇa*), reflecting (*manana*), practicing (*nididhyāsana*) and weeping put in prayer (because of the inability to put what is heard into practice), when the mind is thus perfectly purified, then and then only does the dawn of self-knowledge suddenly break forth in a split second as "I am That I am!" Since, as soon as this dawn breaks, the space of Self-consciousness is found, through the clear knowledge of the Reality, to be beginningless, natural and eternal, even the effort of attending to Self ceases then! To abide thus, having nothing more to do and nothing further to achieve, is alone the real and supreme state.[73]

73. Sri Sadhu Om, *A Light on the Teaching of Bhagavan Sri Ramana Maharshi* (Asheboro, NC: AHAM Publications, 2002).

Purification of the Breath and *Tapas*

Closely related to the topic of *kriyās* is the so-called "fire of yoga" or *tapas*. As we meditate, we are supposed to be able to burn our karma in the fire of yoga, roast our *saṃskāras*, and purify our breath. But what does the word "fire" signify? And what does the word "purify" actually mean?

Purification of the Breath

It is common to hear the analogy that when we practice yoga, we are purifying our body and mind just as gold melted in fire is separated from its impurities. Although it is a beautiful analogy, it does not tell us much. To understand how purification in yoga works, we first need to better understand *prāna*.

Prāna, in its most basic sense, is our life energy. *Prāna* comes into the body from many sources: from the sun, from the air we breathe, from the food we eat. Within the body there are several different types of *prāna* that govern different functions, including aiding digestion, evacuation of waste, distribution of vitality, and so forth. The five principal *prānas* are: *prāna*, *apāna*, *udāna*, *samāna*, and *vyāna*. All *prānas* are ultimately one, and *prāna* itself is a grosser form of Shakti.

Once *prāna* enters the body, it is distributed through our network of *nāḍīs* that resemble our physical nervous system. As we go through ordinary life, some of our *nāḍīs* naturally become blocked, just as an artery can become blocked. But here, the blockage is not caused by a foreign substance (like plaque), but by the interruption or narrowing of the smooth flow of energy through a channel. The blockage in the *nāḍī* can be caused by emotional disturbances (excessive anger, depression, negative thoughts) and by unhealthy living (smoking, excessive consumption of meat, alcohol, nicotine, or through excessive loss of our sexual fluids). When our breathing becomes weak (people who do not exercise and sit all day long are known to breathe using only a small upper portion of their lungs), the *nāḍīs* are also affected. In short, many things can cause reductions in the flow of *prāna* throughout the *nāḍis*, and in yoga it is said that the root of most diseases can be traced back to blocked *nāḍis*.

The system of *nāḍis*, which are traditionally numbered at 72,000, have three principal channels: the *iḍā*, *pingala*, and *sushumṇā*. *Iḍā* is considered lunar or cool and runs down through the left nostril. *Pingala* is considered solar or hot and runs down through the right nostril. *Sushumṇā* is the central channel, and runs straight up along the spine. (Note: Sri Bhagawan Nityananda revealed the *sushumṇā* as the sun [red in color], the *iḍā* as the moon [blue in color], and the pingala as the star [green in color]).[74]

Some texts envision the *iḍā* and *pingala* channels criss-crossing each other, while others envision them running parallel along each side of the *sushumṇā*. These different interpretations are not really material to our practice of yoga. The point is that our breath flows through either *iḍā*, *pingala*, or both. Specifically, we usually pull some air in with both nostrils but the primary flow of *prāna* tends to occur either through the *iḍā* or *pingala nāḍi*, alternating every ninety minutes or so.

Being able to make the *prāna* flow through both *iḍā* and *pingala* simultaneously (equalizing the breath) is one of the required accomplishments in the early stages of meditation. In fact, it is the first stage of what it means to "purify" the breath. Although there are specific physical breathing techniques that encourage the *prāna* to equalize, if in meditation we establish a strong intention for the Shakti and grace of the Guru to spontaneously unfold everything we need, then all yogic processes will occur automatically. In other words, we let the Shakti determine what we need, when we need it, and to what degree. Our sole job is to strive to unite our identity with the mantra or to penetrate directly into our I-feeling,

74. *Chidākāsh Gīta*, verse 2.

and as soon as the *prāna* begins to equalize, we will begin to experience the transcendental bliss of the Self.

As we all know, the breath and the mind are intimately connected. When the mind is calm, the breath is slow and steady. When the mind is agitated, the breath is shallow and rapid.

Since the mantra itself is a vibration of Shakti, as soon as we harmonize the mantra to our breath, we begin to draw down Shakti into the body through the *brahmarandhra*, the cranial aperture at the top of the skull. As the Shakti accumulates, it begins to affect the vibration of *prāna* contained within the breath. More precisely, the *prāna* begins to vibrate at a higher or more subtle frequency, if you will, and this refinement of *prāna* is also referred to as the purification of the breath. (It must be stressed that simply joining a mantra to the breath will not affect the *prāna* to any great extent unless the mantra is repeated with proper awareness and technique.)

As the *prāna* is vitalized by the Shakti of the mantra, it begins to flow powerfully through the *nādīs*. Over time, the Shakti clears all the blockages within the network of *nādīs*, and as we meditate with greater and greater subtlety, the *prāna* becomes highly refined, purifying our three bodies (physical, subtle, and causal). As a matter of fact, the Shakti rejuvenates our inner organs, our cells, our blood, our bone marrow, and so on. The numinous glow that is sometimes exhibited by yogins is due to the presence of Shakti and unrestricted *prāna* coursing through their bodies. Accordingly, the purification of the breath does not refer to the air that we inhale and exhale, but to the vibration of *prāna* within the breath.

In addition to its effects on our body, refining or elevating the vibration of *prāna* is extremely important in how it affects our thought stream. As discussed earlier, the actual work of stilling the mind is not accomplished by brute force. Instead, the vibration of the mantra and its association with pure Consciousness is what holds the power to quiet the mind.

As our restless thoughts begin to settle under the influence of the mantra or by us keeping our attention on our I-feeling, our breath also begins to grow longer and slower. In this way, the quieter the mind becomes, the longer the breath grows until it becomes so long and slow that the space between each inhalation and exhalation begins to widen. Eventually, when the twin currents of *prāna* and *apāna* collect at the back of the throat and merge into *sushumnā*, inner breathing begins (pranic breathing), and the outer breath disappears altogether. From the outside, it appears as if the yogin is no longer breathing but has somehow managed to stay alive, and in fact this is exactly what happens. At this point, the *udāna prāna* working within the *sushumnā nādī* takes over the functions from *prāna* and *apāna*, making it possible for the *Prāna* Kundalini Shakti to flash upwards like a reverse lightning bolt, piercing all the chakras.

To achieve the merging of the *prāna* and *apāna* into *sushumnā* is the destination of every yogin, whether they know it or not. In this way, the purification of the breath is fully achieved when our breathing becomes so long and slow that the *prānas* alternating between the left and right channels collect at the back of the throat and slip down into *sushumnā nādī*.

The Fire of Yoga

At a basic level, simply resisting bad impulses or desires by replacing them with positive thoughts creates a natural mental friction that is considered yogic "heat." We all know how difficult it is to rebuff old, ingrained habits, and this mental resistance to temptation is an ascetic practice that relies on our willpower (which is why we sometimes fail).

As yogins, it is our duty to strive to eradicate negative habits, the purpose being to preserve the divine Shakti we are accumulating through our meditation practice. If we work hard at meditating but then turn around and dissipate all our precious energy by indulging every whim and desire, we will be taking one step forward and two steps back. Yet it is important to note that simply being deprived of something we have a strong desire for does not in and of itself create yogic heat (think of incarcerated inmates who strongly desire one thing or another). Instead, our resistance to the pull of the senses has to be volitional *and* filled with the awareness of the Self. Only then will our self-restraint become purificatory in nature. This is *tapasyā* (ascetic practice), but even this type of practice is not the real yogic heat.

Real yogic heat is proportional to the degree of concentration of mind that we achieve. As our mind becomes one-pointed through mantra repetition or by fixing it directly in our I-consciousness, the pure Awareness that fuels the mantra begins to shine in our intellect, which normally reflects our mass of convoluted thoughts. In this way, the intellect is like a prism that is completely colored either by body-mind identification (grey clouds) or by pure Awareness (bright blue sky). The rising of pure Awareness in the screen of the intellect is the real yogic heat.

In practical terms, the "friction" between the breath and the mantra is what causes yogic heat. (A common analogy is that the mantra and the breath are sticks that when rubbed together ignite a fire.) The "heat" being referred to is the mantra's intense vibratory nature, or more precisely, the pure Awareness that is in fact the mantra. Alternatively, the "heat" is the centering of our attention directly into our I-consciousness. Absorption into the mantra or into Self-attention destroys the stream of thoughts, roasts our old impressions, and finally even burns away most of our stored karma, removing us from the endless cycle of transmigration.

Ultimately, yogic heat is the very center of pure Awareness. Its power completely changes our body right down to the cellular level and utterly transforms our mind. In this light, Self-attention is actually the real alchemical power that transforms the iron of the ordinary mind into the gold of pure, divine Awareness. The Shakti that accumulates as a result of right effort is spoken of in terms of a divine fire because it burns everything to a crisp, until only the stainless blue sky of Consciousness remains.

CHAPTER SEVEN

Meditation Phases and Landscapes

The concept of creating a map of meditation phases is justifiably controversial. After all, there cannot be any singular or universal map that perfectly describes the interior stages of meditation. Accounts of what transpires after we close our eyes vary greatly between traditions and individual yogins, which comes as no surprise since our inner experiences are, to a great extent, shaped by our individual storehouse of mental impressions. Nevertheless, it is possible to piece together a working model of the inner stages of meditation based on the writings of sages and yogins. At the very least, two key events or milestones emerge that appear common to most meditators. What happens between these milestones is unique to each person.

When we study various meditation maps, the descriptions tend to be framed around a particular aspect of reality. For instance, some yogins describe the journey as a progression of purification starting with the physical body, down to the subtle body, then further down into the causal body until one's awareness finally reaches the transcendental fourth state, or *turīya*. Other writings focus on how the vibration of sound (and awareness) become progressively subtle, descending from the mouth into the throat chakra, then down into the heart space, and finally into the navel chakra until the dawning of pure Awareness arises. Yet others focus mostly on the infinite variety of *kriyās* that unfold under the command of the Shakti or on how the *prāna* becomes refined until it merges into the central channel. Other texts cast their light on the objects of contemplation (as Patañjali does in his *Yoga Sūtra*), explaining how what we concentrate on becomes progressively subtle until both the seer and the seen finally merge and disappear. Yet other traditions, such as Vedanta, tend to bypass meditative descriptions altogether, focusing exclusively on the end target of pure Awareness. In this way, meditation maps are akin to the parable of the four blind men who touched different parts of an elephant, describing the same animal in completely different ways.

Nevertheless, after a little study it becomes apparent that a few common milestones do exist along the way, enabling us to formulate a simple but useful map of what lies down the road. Knowing what we can reasonably expect as we progress in meditation is important, for otherwise how will we be able to conceptualize an end point to our journey or sense how far we have come along the path? Moreover, having an idea of what awaits us might save us from failing to recognize important signposts or from reacting improperly to various mystical phenomena, especially of the frightening variety.

Here we realize the enormous benefits of uniting the wisdom that Tantric and Vedantic methods have to offer. Although at the philosophical level there are stark contrasts between both traditions, at the practical level a thorough Tantric understanding of the workings of the Kundalini Shakti, the *nāḍīs*, and the *kriyās*, combined with Sri Ramana's command to focus on nothing but our I-sense, allows us to establish a deeply informed and highly stable foundation that results in profound meditative absorption. If and when mystical experiences do present themselves, we will not be thrown off base. Instead, we will be able to understand and appreciate them, while at the same time maintaining our focus on our formless I-sense.

I note that a proposed meditation map stands in stark contrast to some teachers who show disdain for any discussion of states or phases. They claim that since all states are rooted in duality and are limiting by nature, paying attention to them runs contrary to the primary goal of meditation, which is to break free from all states and rest in perfect stillness. Now while it is true that perfect Self-awareness is beyond all states and phenomena, it is not true to claim that we can become established in Self-awareness without passing through a number of states and phases, at least for the vast majority of us. Accordingly, in my view it is important to understand the meditative phases that are likely to transpire, with the caveat that we should not allow ourselves to become sidetracked by them.

For this section I draw from two primary sources: my own direct experience and the teachings of the great Swami Lakshmanjoo. Our meditation map is divided into five phases, with two of them representing major milestones or breakthrough events.

Phase I: Settling into Our Posture, Mantra Repetition, and Focusing Attention at the Center of Each Repetition

When we first start our practice, much of our initial effort is simply mastering our commitment to meditate on a daily basis. It might feel strange at first to force ourselves out of bed before dawn when there's no early flight or urgent meeting but simply the duty to sit on our cushion and close our eyes. As stated earlier, rising for meditation should never feel like a chore. Although our desire to sleep may sometimes get the better of us, if we remember our goal of experiencing the bliss of Self-awareness, we can roll out of bed full of enthusiasm.

Once we are established in our new routine, the focus shifts to growing comfortable with our sitting posture and learning to properly unite with our mantra or centering on the awareness between each repetition.

At first we may have to deal with physical pains, such as cramps in our ankles or legs. Our backs may hurt from sitting on a cushion that is either too high or too low. In time, however, we will overcome these obstacles to the point that we can sit in total comfort for a least an hour (allowing for minor adjustments in our posture).

Likewise, we will notice that we become proficient at repeating our mantra for long periods of time. Not only do we become intimately familiar with the foreign sounding Sanskrit syllables that turn in our mouth, but we come to love and ultimately identify completely with the sacred sound until the mantra begins to reveal its hidden and secret power. It is here that we tend to make a subconscious choice of how to work with the mantra, either listening intently to the sound until we merge into it, or using the repetitions as rails to allow us to penetrate into the Awareness that lies at the center.

This initial phase of meditation can last for months, years, or an entire lifetime, with variations in progress usually governed by our degree of devotion to God and by how strong our desire to merge into pure Awareness is. As Patañjali states in his *Yoga Sūtra*, "It [samādhi] is nearest to those whose desire [for samādhi] is intensely strong."[75]

Phase II: First Wave of Kriyās

As we practice posture, breath, mantra, and awareness, as long as we are filled with a sincere longing to surrender into pure Consciousness, that feeling itself is enough to eventually awaken the Kundalini Shakti and initiate her various *kriyās*. Likewise, if we go about our day repeating our mantra or focusing on our I-feeling with proper awareness, then we will be engaging in the highest level of bodily purification.

In this way, purifying the body does not mean keeping it physically clean and observing dietary restrictions (avoiding meat, alcohol, nicotine, and other harmful products). While these are strongly encouraged, such do's and don'ts represent only the most superficial level of purification. True physical and mental purification unfolds when we practice feeling

75. *Yoga Sūtra*, 1:21-22.

that our body and the world are nothing but consciousness (a practice that is only truly possible after we have made contact with the Self through daily meditation), or, alternatively, when we identify strictly with our I-sense to the exclusion of all else. Otherwise, absent any direct experience, any talk of being pure Consciousness is nothing but wishful thinking.

On the other hand, once we make contact with the Self, it becomes possible to touch upon the reality that everything is consciousness. It is as if we toss our body and mind into pure Awareness in the same way that we toss a penny into a fountain. It only takes a split second to move into pure Consciousness, and the results can sometimes be felt at the physical level. For instance, on one occasion as I stepped out of the shower, I became keenly aware that everything was consciousness, and when my foot touched the floor I experienced my body as completely weightless. After a few steps, my awareness returned to normal, along with my body's density.

As we continue to harmonize our breath to the mantra, these two great sticks of yoga rub together, allowing the fire of Awareness at the center of our breath to blaze forth. In this initial stage, any number of physical *kriyās* can take place.

We may also continue to experience physical or psychological *kriyās* outside of our formal meditation session, such as heat, pressure, visions of light, persistent thoughts, and so forth. Over time they all settle down, leaving the mind and intellect bright and crystal clear. Our memory tends to improve, and we may notice feeling greater equipoise with more patience, compassion, and contentment manifesting for no apparent reason.

In time, as the breath becomes longer and the mind quieter due to the presence of the mantra, we may feel the very first stirrings of divine bliss and peace rising from within. This first contact with authentic meditative bliss is extremely important, for it proves to us that the Self is real since the quality or "taste" of divine bliss is so remotely different and superior to anything we have ever experienced before. Moreover, once we touch bliss, our eagerness to meditate increases a hundredfold.

As we continue to meditate day after day, more often than not we will begin to experience greater stillness and refinement in the vibration of the mantra. During this phase it is common to experience our muscles spontaneously moving us into *mūla, uḍḍiyāna*, and *jalandhara bandha*.[76]

As stated above, during this phase a number of phenomena may unfold both in and out of meditation. For example, we may be able to see pulsating white light shooting out of our eyes, hands, and feet when we turn off the lights in our room. Or we may begin to experience dreams that feel hyper-real, with sages and divine deities visiting us to bless us with messages. In short, as we draw down Shakti, any number of experiences can manifest (or none at all). The point is not to accumulate experiences, which takes us away from the goal, but simply to understand that mystical experiences are quite common when we are meditating properly. Conversely, if we do not have experiences, as long as we detect a gradual quieting of the mind, we should have faith that we are making progress and that everything is progressing exactly as it should.

As our ability to quiet our mind gradually increases, our *kriyās* will begin to calm down, and we may find that we have reached a thoughtless and blissful space where we are barely able to notice the passage of time. Our breath may become extremely slow, so that it almost feels as if we are not breathing at all. At other times we may experience our inhalation or exhalation become suspended in what is termed *kumbhaka,*

---

76. In *mūla bandha* the perineum muscles are drawn upward, in *uḍḍiyāna bandha* the abdominal muscles are drawn in and upward, and in *jalandhara bandha* the chin is locked into the suprasternal notch. It is important to emphasize that all of these locks transpire automatically in meditation under the inspiration of the Kundalini Shakti.

and that we are "breathing" through the central channel.[77] At this level it becomes very easy to meditate for two hours at a stretch, and we may notice that we begin to feel sleepy near the end of our session, to the point where we are overtaken by a strong desire to lie down. Such grogginess indicates that our meditation is progressing extremely well, and it signals that we are nearing the end of this phase.

Phase III: First Milestone: Breaking Through the Sleep Barrier

After uniting strongly with our mantra and settling into our I-consciousness, there comes a time during the last five, ten, or twenty minutes of our session where we are overcome with an intense and almost irresistible desire to sleep. This heaviness is a sure sign that our mind is becoming steady and one-pointed and that we are coming close to piercing the space between waking and sleeping, which leads directly into what is called *tandrā*, *nidrā*, or *turīya*.[78]

In my own case, for about a month I was unable to remain conscious, actually falling asleep no matter how hard I tried. But with a firm resolve I set an intention to stay awake, reaching a point soon after where the vibration of Shakti grew very intense. In fact it felt as if my I-consciousness had reached the edge of an "abyss," and that if I went any deeper into meditation I would fall into a void in which I would die or disappear altogether. As I reached this formless "edge," great waves of fear swept over me, and I would pull back from my

---

77. *Kumbhaka* is of two kinds: internal, where the breath is suspended after the inhalation, or external, where it is suspended after exhalation. In our system, *kumbhaka* occurs naturally, guided by the will of the Shakti, and is not consciously performed.

78. Swami Lakshmanjoo states that when we penetrate into the awareness between any two points, such as waking and dreaming, dreaming and deep sleep, the pause between two thoughts or two breaths, and so on, that we enter directly into *turīya*, the fourth state. See Hughes, *Self Realization in Kashmir Shaivism*.

one-pointedness of mind, which effectively threw me out of meditation. Days went by and each time I reached this point, I pulled back, unable to overcome my fear until I realized that if dying in this way meant merging into a greater Awareness, then I had nothing to fear.

Armed with this shield of trust and surrender, I bowed to my Guru and vowed that I would not pull back no matter what happened, and the following day when I reached this very intense point of stillness, I was finally able to let go and "throw myself" into it, at which point I emerged into the state of *tandrā*.

Phase IV: Passage Through Tandrā

The state of *tandrā* is where a yogin becomes awestruck, for he or she enters into a universe as vivid and real as the world we live in. As Swami Lakshmanjoo teaches, once the mind penetrates into *tandrā*, the ability to move one's body ends. The hands cannot move, the eyelids remain closed, and so on. It is similar to entering into the dream state, with the difference that what is perceived in *tandrā* is hyper-real. Moreover, while in ordinary dream state our mind is scattered, in *tandrā* the mind is highly concentrated.

Swami Lakshmanjoo does not use the word *tandrā*, but refers directly to *turīya* to describe the vivid plane of consciousness between waking and sleep. Others have explained *tandrā* as a state that emerges halfway between deep sleep and *turīya*, here meant as the final transcendental state of consciousness.[79]

Within *tandrā* many kinds of visions, sounds, landscapes, and fragrances manifest before us. As we draw down Shakti, our *prāna* is refined and our breathing evens out, causing awareness of our subtle body to increase. When the mind

79. Swami Muktananda, *Satsang with Baba: Questions and Answers with Swami Muktananda*, vol. 4 (Oakland, CA: SYDA Foundation, 1978).

becomes sufficiently one-pointed, our external organs of action and perception are shut out, and we cross into the dream-like world of *tandrā*. But unlike the ordinary world of dreams, which are fragmented and unstable, the worlds within *tandrā* are solid. Moreover, what transpires in *tandrā* is a direct continuation of our *sādhanā* (unlike most common dreams), because in *tandrā* the purification of our mind advances at great speed. Swami Lakshmanjoo writes:

> In the state of *turīya* you mentally perceive the presence of the five subtle elements (*tanmātras*), but you must not indulge in these five attractions. You must completely ignore them and settle ever more deeply into your own one-pointed awareness. This settling is called *pratyāhāra*. It is the winding up of the external world and the entering into the supreme internal world. No darkness exists there. It is light itself.[80]

When I emerged into *tandrā*, my chin was locked in *jalandhara bandha*, and the first reality I experienced was to see myself sitting in my cross-legged meditation posture. I was staring down at my legs, but curiously, I was not wearing the same clothes; the carpet beneath me was totally different, and when I looked up, the room around me was also different. Everything felt hyper-real, but after only a few seconds I was thrown out of *tandrā*.

From there onwards, each time I sat down to meditate, around the fiftieth minute of my session I would penetrate into *tandrā*, and the scenes grew more varied and complex. I saw forests before me or would find myself standing in a courtyard adorned with palm trees.

---

80. The *tanmātras* are the subtle elements of sight, sound, touch, taste, and smell. Swami Lakshmanjoo quoted in Hughes, *Self Realization in Kashmir Shaivism*.

Although all the scenes were pleasant, they were short-lived, for the vibration of energy was so intense that I could not sustain it for more than a few seconds before my meditation session would abruptly come to an end. As I continued to meditate with great enthusiasm, my ability to remain in *tandrā* increased, and some of my visions began to cross over into this world. On one occasion, while in *tandrā* a radiant blue flame appeared before me, about two to three inches in height, and as I stared at it intensely, my eyes suddenly opened. But instead of just seeing my room, I was amazed to see the blue flame burning right over my desk, making me realize that it is quite true that the visions encountered in *tandrā* can cross over into our external reality (which explains how some of the more forceful visions yogins experience transpire while their eyes are wide open). What happens in these situations is that we do not actually exit *tandrā* when we open our eyes. Because the waking state is supported by *tandrā*, which is its substrate, opened-eyed visions indicate that the normally hidden state of *tandrā* has commingled with our ordinary waking state.

As we stabilize our ability to enter and remain in *tandrā*, three types or levels of visions emerge: the first is a field of random images and visions that have no correlation with reality but which are soon followed by visions of actual events occurring in distant places, that is, clairvoyance develops. The second type of visions are of events that are yet to unfold. Finally, at its most developed stage, the yogin in *tandrā* experiences visions of traveling to other subtle planes of existence, including heavenly and hellish realms.[81] In *tandrā* we may be visited by saints and sages, receive messages that concern our *sādhanā*, or develop a strong intuitive perception.

81. Swami Muktananda, *Satsang with Baba: Questions and Answers with Swami Muktananda*, vol. 1 (Ganeshpuri, India: Gurudev Siddha Peeth, 1974).

Entry into *tandrā* marks what Swami Lakshmanjoo calls an internal voyage that will be "long and arduous," saying that "this path is torturous like the path of a maze or labyrinth."[82] There is no telling whether we will remain in *tandrā* for months or years before reaching the next stage. And while we may be struck with wonder at the divine sights, sounds, and fragrances of the worlds we visit, the scriptures extol us to keep our attention firm and collected on our I-consciousness. Sri Ramana warned seekers to outright ignore all visions since they are nothing but objects before us that promote duality and take us away from the goal of formless Self-awareness.[83] At the same time, many blessings are received while journeying through *tandrā*, so our attitude should be one of grateful acknowledgement and surrender for whatever transpires.

As an aside, our necessary passage through *tandrā* sheds further light on why the *Vijñāna Bhairava*, whose contemplations make it seem as if we can pass into supreme Consciousness in the blink of an eye, should properly be understood as a manual for highly accomplished yogins.

While in *tandrā*, not all of our visions will be pleasant or uplifting. All yogic traditions speak of a passage through terrible sights and sounds and of having to face apocalyptic scenes, such as the burning of our house or room, visions of hell or of hellish forms, frightening howls and screams, and so on. On this point Swami Lakshmanjoo confirms that such visions happen in *turīya*, but if they are endured and tolerated, they will eventually pass. In fact, they must be tolerated if we are to reach the next stage of absorption, and Swamiji teaches that to get through such terrifying visions we must focus on our breath while repeating our mantra with great faith and devotion. It is common during these visions to feel certain

---

82. Swami Lakshmanjoo quoted in Hughes, *Self Realization in Kashmir Shaivism*.
83. Sri Ramana, quoted in Godman, *Be As You Are*.

that we are going to die, but the feeling should be counteracted by the equal certainty that we are going to live. Swami Lakshmanjoo writes:

> When the aspirant desires to move from individuality to universality, all of these experiences occur because individuality has to be shaken off. When this movement toward universality begins, this kind of struggle takes place.[84]

It is important to point out that our passage through *tandrā* is not constantly filled with perceptions, meaning that within any given meditation session we may spend part of our time immersed in formless awareness and another part navigating through *tandrā*.

Phase V: Second Milestone: Yogic Death, Merging of the Breath into the Central Channel, Rise of the Kundalini, Krama Mudrā, and Liberation

As the hideous forms pass, we near the next milestone of our meditative journey. In this critical phase of meditation, the breath begins to lose its natural momentum, making it difficult to breathe and causing us to choke. An intuitive knowing that the breath is about to stop comes over us, and our breath begins to coagulate at the back of the throat until it stops functioning. Instead of flowing in and out, the breath now feels as if it's rotating like a whirlpool in a fixed spot at the back of the soft palate. Swami Lakshmanjoo teaches that the breath collects at the *lambikā*, a confluence of four passages that meet on the right side of the throat. Normally, two of the four passages are open during normal breathing, but when the breath is about to stop, those close and the other two open, "capturing" the breath so that it whirls in a fixed spot.[85]

84. Swami Lakshmanjoo and Hughes, *Kashmir Shaivism*.
85. Ibid.

As this point Swamiji again advises us to fix our minds on our mantra and to steady ourselves as much as possible. We must have absolute faith in the Guru and in the Self to move forward, for the yogin who hesitates throws himself out of this process.

With our breath whirling faster and faster, the feeling of choking increases until our mouth becomes crooked and our face shows all the signs of death. Here we must do everything in our power to tolerate the waves of fear, surrendering fully to the will of God. If we are able to persevere, our breathing stops altogether and our breath rushes down the central channel until it reaches the *mūlādhāra* chakra, causing the latter to move with great force and sound in a clockwise direction. As our breath penetrates the *mūlādhāra*, we experience a crawling sensation, like ants moving. Then an intense feeling of pleasure ensues and the Kundalini Shakti rises up in a flash to the next chakra, which also begins to whirl with great force and sound, also in a clockwise direction. The process repeats itself all the way up until the Kundalini pierces the *ājñā* chakra between the eyebrows. At this point the yogin exhales once. Then the breathing stops again, and the Kundalini rises from *ājñā* to *brahmarandhra* at the top of the skull, piercing the *sahasrāra* chakra, causing the yogin to exhale again. It is only from this moment on that we become possessed of the eight great yogic powers.[86]

From this point forward, we are very close to achieving final enlightenment. If we have come this far, we will undergo the process of *krama mudrā*, whereby our eyes open and close repeatedly until the interior experience of God consciousness

---

86. The eight yogic powers are: *aṇimā*, the power of reducing one's body to a minute size; *laghima*, the power of becoming very light; *mahima*, the power to create an enormous body; *garima*, the power to become extremely heavy; *isitvam*, the power to control the entire universe; *vasitvam*, the power of charisma and attractiveness; *prakamyam*, the power to control all bodily functions (such as hunger); and *vyapti*, the power to know anything that is occurring in the universe.

is unified with the external world. In other words, the process of *krama mudrā* is what allows us to truly experience the outer world as made up of nothing but pure being, consciousness, and bliss. Swamiji teaches that each time the process of coming out and going in occurs, it fills us with more and more ecstasy. When *krama mudrā* is complete, which can take anywhere between one to hundreds of meditation sessions, we emerge fully established in the highest and permanent state of *sahaja samādhi*, or natural absorption in the Self. In other words, once *krama mudrā* stabilizes, we are properly liberated and all notions of practice are over. After rising from our meditation seat, we remain permanently established in Self-awareness despite the fact that our differentiated perception of the world remains, just as a mirage is still seen even after we realize it to be a mere optical illusion.[87]

Swami Lakshmanjoo cautions that the rise of the Kundalini Shakti may not proceed all the way up to the *ājñā* chakra, but that it may stop after reaching any of the lower chakras. If we are thrown out of meditation at any point along the way, we should simply try again. The rise of the Kundalini all the way up to the *ājñā* chakra is determined by the degree of devotion and surrender we have acquired. If spiritual longing is still mixed with worldly desires, then the Shakti may only rise partway.[88]

Likewise, even if the Kundalini manages to pierce the *ājñā* chakra, the rise from *ājñā* to *sahasrāra* is even more difficult to accomplish. Our previous focus on Awareness must have been very strong, otherwise after piercing the *ājñā* chakra we will be thrown back into external awareness and prevented from rising any further, although it goes without saying that any yogin who manages to reach this stage is far from being an ordinary person.

Since how high the Kundalini is willing or destined to

87. Swami Lakshmanjoo and Hughes, *Kashmir Shaivism.*
88. Ibid.

ascend is for the most part beyond our control, we gain nothing by worrying about it. As always, our sole task is to remain centered on our I-feeling and surrender to the processes of yoga to the fullest extent of our capacity.

It bears mentioning that for a very select group of highly advanced yogins, the rise of the Kundalini does not unfold progressively, as in the rise of *Prāna* Kundalini, but in a single flash. In the rise of *Chit* Kundalini, the sacred energy flashes upward from *mūlādhāra* to *ājñā* chakra, bypassing the individual rotations of each chakra. Swami Lakshmanjoo teaches that *Chit* Kundalini only manifests for those individuals who are completely absorbed in their *sādhanā* and are devoid of worldly attachments or desires. If, like most seekers, we crave both worldly and spiritual fulfillment, then our Kundalini will rise by piercing one chakra at a time as described above in the process of *Prāna* Kundalini.[89]

Closing Observations

Framing our practice within the five meditation phases allows us to better understand what lies behind us and what lies ahead. The two milestones of breaking through the sleep barrier and penetrating into *tandrā*, followed by the experience of our yogic death and the lightning rise of the Kundalini, serve as toll bridges that let us know exactly where we are. So no matter how long it takes us to work through the initial accumulation of Shakti and corresponding *kriyās*, or how long we roam through the inner worlds after crossing into *tandrā*, we will not feel lost. And until we are fortunate enough to experience the stopping of the breath and the union of *prāna* and *apāna* in the *sushumnā nāḍī*, followed by the piercing of all the chakras, these milestones stand as sentinels that prevent us from falling into the erroneous belief (due to the very high states experienced in *tandrā*) that we have attained complete Self-awareness before we actually

89. Ibid.

have. Likewise, all the discussion found in books about the chakras "opening" or being pierced by focusing on them or breathing into them do not represent the true piercing of the wheels of energy but are at most preliminary *kriyās* of one type or another.

As noted earlier, the yogic path is never linear in the sense that even after attaining *tandrā*, we may sit for individual sessions that keep us bobbing at the surface of the mind or pull us deeply into formless stillness, only to return to the visual elements of *tandrā* at a later date and only for a small portion of our session. As we shall explore below, many of the levels of *samādhi* presented in Patañjali's *Yoga Sūtra* transpire within the state of *tandrā*.

Finally, we should also note that as we move into deeper states of consciousness, constant vigilance is required since territory that is gained can just as easily be lost. If our daily meditation practice is discontinued for whatever reason, depending on how far we have strayed in controlling our senses and for how long we have stopped, we might discover to our great disappointment that we have to begin almost anew, with the Shakti even reviving some of the old *kriyās* that had already subsided (because the affected *nāḍīs* need to be purified once again).

Needless to say, the duration of each phase or of any given *kriyā* varies from person to person. What may take a person one month to cross may take another a full year. And since we have little control over the pace of our progress (our contribution being limited to the depth of our devotion, eagerness to meditate, and proper technique), comparing ourselves to others is more than just a waste of time, it is flat out detrimental to our *sādhanā*. Likewise, sitting down with an expectation that we should pierce the sleep barrier into *tandrā* or experience this or that *kriyā* is a sure way to halt all progress. Although it is good to be aware of such milestones, we should settle into each meditation session free of hopes, desires, or expectations, since these are the very things that stop the Shakti from unfolding. In my own case, I meditated every morning with the simple intent to absorb myself in pure, thoughtless Awareness, and the piercing of the sleep barrier happened quite unexpectedly after my body and mind had undergone a sufficient amount of purification. In fact, it was only after attaining *tandrā* that I understood what had transpired after I stumbled upon certain passages from the writings of Swami Muktananda. Since reality is formless and exists only in the present moment, our sole task is to fix all our attention on our I-feeling and surrender as much as possible to the indwelling Lord. If we persevere with great love and devotion, doing our best to empty our mind of all expectation, there is no reason for us not to be blessed with swift progress.

CHAPTER EIGHT

Samādhi as Described in Patañjali's *Yoga Sūtra*

Since this book is informed by Hindu tradition, a discussion of Patañjali's *Yoga Sūtra*, which contains one of the most important and well-known classifications of the various levels of *samādhi*, is helpful. For our purposes we will briefly touch on how Patañjali's classification of the different types of *samādhi* fit or correspond to the five-step framework proposed above. If, as per our system, it is true that both the rise of the Kundalini and the piercing of the chakras unfold immediately after the breath merges into the central channel, then at what point in our meditative journey do we experience the different states of absorption described in the *Yoga Sūtra*?

Prior to *samādhi*, which is the final stage in his eightfold system, Patañjali discusses *dhāraṇā* and *dhyāna*.[90] In essence, *dhāraṇā* refers to the act of willfully concentrating on a single thought. When we first sit down to meditate, our minds are flooded with all kinds of thoughts, and our effort is aimed at keeping only one thought at the center of our attention (usually our mantra or the image of our Guru). We gently let go of all other thoughts and try to stay focused on repeating our mantra. This continuous effort to concentrate on a single thought is called *dhāraṇā*.

90. Patañjali's eight limbs of yoga are: *yama* (abstentions), *niyama* (observances), *āsana* (posture), *prāṇāyāma* (control of the *prāna*), *pratyāhāra* (withdrawal of the mind), *dhāraṇā* (concentration), *dhyāna* (meditation), and *samādhi* (absorption).

Eventually, when we succeed at holding onto one continuous thought so that it flows in our mind like an unbroken stream of oil, we enter into what is termed *dhyāna* or meditation proper. It is important to note that at this stage we are still aware of both ourselves and of the one thought before our mind, so there is still a clear duality present: that of the thinker and of the thought before him or her.

As concentration increases, *samādhi*, in its most general sense, manifests when the single object in focus becomes so strong that all awareness of the thinker vanishes, leaving only the object of thought before the field of awareness. In other words, the mind loses awareness of itself when it enters into *samādhi*, collapsing the division between the knower, knowledge, and the object of knowledge. It is also important to point out that the initial levels of *samādhi* are impermanent in nature, meaning that when the yogin emerges from meditation, the mind's awareness of itself as a separate "I" returns immediately. That is why the initial stages of *samādhi*, exalted as they may be, are not tantamount to final Self-realization or liberation.

One of the key differences between Patañjali's and Sri Ramana's approach to meditation is that Patañjali believes that absorption into objects of knowledge must always begin with gross objects, such as an image or mantra, and progress gradually to increasingly subtle objects, such as the vibration of sound or the I-sense. After passing through the most subtle object, which is our I-feeling, we finally reach the true objectless *samādhi* that delivers us into a state of permanent Self-awareness. Sri Ramana, on the other hand, dispenses with the requirement to meditate on external objects of perception, and instead urges us from the start to focus solely on our innate I-feeling.

Patañjali's model is set out below with the following four levels:

1. *Samprajñāta samādhi* (with objects of perception and filled with *sabīja* [with seed or latent impressions]):

   a. *Savitarka* and *nirvitarka* (gross objects);

   b. *Savicāra* and *nirvicāra* (subtle objects);

   c. *Sānanda* (plane of bliss);

   d. *Sasmita* (plane of pure I-ness);

2. *Asamprajñāta samādhi* (no objects of perception but filled with latent impressions);

3. *Nirbīja samādhi* (no objects of perception and devoid of latent impressions);

4. *Dharma-megha samādhi* (cloud of virtue).[91]

As listed above, the *Yoga Sūtra* breaks down objects of perception used as the targets of attention into four levels: *savitarka* and *nirvitarka* (gross objects), *savicāra* and *nirvicāra* (subtle objects), *sānanda* (plane of bliss), and *sasmita* (plane of pure I-ness). Let us examine each type of object of perception more closely.

Samprajñāta Samādhi—Savitarka and *Nirvitarka* (gross objects)

Samprajñāta means *sa* (with) *prajñāta* (consciousness). This is the entry-level *samādhi* where the trinity of knower, knowing, and known collapse and only the object remains in the field of awareness (the known), and whereby the mind loses awareness of itself as an observer. There is clearly a gross object of thought before the mind; it is only that the mind

91. *Yoga Sūtra,* 1:17, 1:18, and 4:30.

has become so focused and fused to the object that the mind seemingly disappears, leaving only the object in the mental field of awareness. Accordingly, when we attain complete unity with our mantra, as discussed in the meditation instructions, we achieve *savitarka samādhi.*

Savitarka objects include gross thoughts, the gross breath, the gross sound of the mantra, the image of the Guru, thought streams, visualizations of the chakras, and even emotions and attitudes such as compassion or devotion. All these are accessible to the beginner and can be placed before the mind during meditation.

After the mind becomes steady in the gross level of *samprajñāta samādhi*, it experiences the true nature of the object before it. On this point Patañjali states that the memory of any object is purified of two lesser types of knowledge: knowledge based on the meaning of words and ordinary knowledge based on the input of the five senses as it relates to any object.[92] When these two types of knowledge are eliminated by mentally fusing into the object through *samādhi*, then the true innate nature of the object begins to shine. It is at this point that we enter into the *nirvitarka* (devoid of gross thought) *samādhi*. In other words, pure and direct knowledge of any object is attained when *savitarka* gives way to *nirvitarka samādhi*. This knowledge is not based on the input of the senses or on the meaning of words used to describe the object. It is a pure knowledge that arises when the mind directly fuses (through concentration) into an object. It amounts to direct cognition without the use of the senses.

Samprajñāta Samādhi—Savicāra and Nirvicāra (subtle objects)

Upon stabilizing in *nirvitarka samādhi*, we emerge into the second level, which is *savicāra samādhi*. Here the process is repeated, but instead of latching onto a gross object of

92. *Yoga Sūtra,* 1:42–43.

perception, we gain access to the subtle aspect of objects (the *tanmātras*) and the very instruments of cognition, which themselves become our objects of concentration. For example, the subtle energy behind the breath, the *prāna*, can become an object of awareness. Or the subtle powers of seeing, hearing, tasting, and smelling themselves become the target of attention. The subtle vibration of mantra, beyond the gross sound of the syllables, can also serve as an object of concentration. The subtle objects that appear in meditation may also be of the nature of divine sounds, fragrances, and other phenomena that pertain to the level of the subtle body. When we completely merge into the subtle object before the mind, we pass into the *nirvicāra* level of *samādhi*.

It is interesting to note that only after we manage to attain the *nirvicāra* level of *samādhi* does Patañjali state that the true dawn of spiritual light takes place as the pure Self begins to reflect more strongly in the intellect.[93]

Samprajñāta Samādhi—Sānanda (plane of bliss)

After the *nirvicāra* level, we emerge into *sānanda samādhi*. In this level, both the gross and subtle forms of objects give way to a plane of bliss that emanates from the causal body beyond the intellect. In *sānanda samādhi*, there is still a perceiver (the limited I-sense) that experiences the vibrations of bliss. For this reason, the bliss at this level remains a subtle object of experience that is rooted in duality and which is less than the highest non-dual bliss of the absolute Self. The bliss felt in *sānanda samādhi* is primarily a result of the mind becoming extremely one-pointed as it moves into a deeper awareness of its own subjectivity.

Although the *sānanda* level of absorption might convey the impression that meditative bliss cannot be experienced until a very high level of yoga is reached, I am happy to report that deep peace and bliss can be experienced even in the

93. *Yoga Sūtra*, 1.47–48.

early stages of practice as soon as the mind attains a certain degree of concentration.

Samprajñāta Samādhi—Sasmita (plane of pure I-ness)

The final level of object-based *samādhi* according to Patañjali is reached when we emerge beyond the plane of bliss into the plane of pure I-ness. In *sasmita samādhi* the mind becomes absorbed in its own innate I-feeling. This is the most subtle object of cognition that the intellect can reflect. Here the I-sense is still the limited sense of individuality that rises like a phantom between the pure Self and the body. In other words, we can state that in *sasmita samādhi* the ego itself becomes the object of concentration.

At this exalted level we merge directly into our own sense of being, which still happens to be blissful. In this sense, bliss is not abandoned; only that a deeper and very subtle shift in concentration takes place from bliss to its perceiver. But even at this high level Patañjali does not allow for a declaration of Self-realization because the *saṃskāra bījas*, the seeds of past mental impressions, have not yet been destroyed.

In terms of how the latent impressions that veil the intellect from pure Awareness are gradually destroyed, every time we pass through *samādhi*, a new mental impression is formed that counteracts and weakens the vast storehouse of mundane, mind-based impressions. This is akin to using a thorn to remove a thorn. In other words, as we gain proficiency in penetrating into a state of *samādhi* through repeated practice, we carry with us newly formed impressions of bliss and stillness that persist throughout our waking state. These new impressions overflow with the light of God, and they create in us an intense craving to keep practicing.

As a result of these blissful impressions, our powers of discrimination (*viveka*) and detachment (*vairāgya*) grow by leaps and bounds, causing our mind to become completely detached from our old desires, attitudes, opinions, and so forth. By constant inattention, our old mental impressions steadily grow weak, while at the same time our newly formed impressions of bliss and stillness grow strong. As we repeatedly dip into *samādhi* during formal meditation, we notice that our previously unbreakable identification to our thoughts, body, and personality finally begins to loosen its grip.

Likewise, the act of concentrating our mind in meditation dislodges many of the old impressions buried deep within our subconscious. When we become conscious of a lingering impression, it greatly weakens the impression's ability to color and influence our mind. Yet reaching the lower levels of *samādhi* does not automatically roast or destroy our latent impressions. For that to occur we must remain steadfast in *samādhi* for long periods of time until we are able to reach the final stage of *nirbīja samādhi*.

Asamprajñāta Samādhi (no objects of perception but filled with latent impressions)

For our purposes, we will not delve deeply into an analysis of *asamprajñāta samādhi* found in *Yoga Sūtra*, 1:18. Briefly, *asamprajñāta samādhi* indicates a mind in an objectless state of absorption that still retains its storehouse of latent impressions. In this *samādhi* the limited I-sense (the ego) is completely transcended, but the yogin does not emerge into full Self-realization due to the presence of lingering *saṃskāras* (latent impressions). This begs the question: Is it possible to transcend the ego while *saṃskāras* remain? I would argue that as long as *saṃskāras* are present, the ego has not really been transcended. Another angle of approach is that in *asamprajñāta samādhi* the ego is not actually transcended; instead, the ego falls into abeyance as the yogin penetrates directly into the causal body, which is pure subjectivity devoid of any objective cognitions. Either way, when thinking about the levels that make up *samādhi*, it is easier and more practical to envision absorption into the I-sense (*sasmita samādhi*) leading directly into *nirbīja samādhi*, where both the ego and latent impressions are simultaneously transcended.

As we meditate on our I-sense, the latent impressions of our blissful, formless absorption grow stronger and stronger, uprooting any remaining impressions that promote identification to our body and mind. With continued practice, every opposing impression gradually burns away until the pure Self is able to shine in the intellect without stain. It is only when the final *saṃskāras* are burned away that the yogin enters the state of *nirbīja samādhi*, or *samādhi* devoid of all latent impressions.

Nirbīja Samādhi (no objects of perception and devoid of latent impressions)

In *nirbīja samādhi*, pure Awareness is able to illumine the intellect free of any obscuring influence. This *samādhi* is experienced as an undivided expanse of perfect Awareness, bliss, and peace. In this way, *nirbīja samādhi* is essentially Self-realization, though Patañjali still makes room for one final level of *samādhi*. Although in *nirbīja samādhi* the last of the mental impressions have been destroyed by the power of Awareness, Patañjali states that final liberation only occurs when the yogin gives up any attachment to even remaining in this highest state of consciousness-bliss. In other words, the yogin must still exercise detachment toward this high state of enlightenment. It is only then that the yogin passes into the final state of *dharma-megha samādhi* and finally emerges into Reality proper.[94]

Dharma-Megha Samādhi (Cloud of Virtue)

Not much can be written about this final level except to say that it is supposed to represent complete liberation from any taint of duality, however subtle, and from the mechanisms (like mental impressions and the *gunas*) that allow duality to assert itself in the first place.

94. *Yoga Sūtra*, 4:29–30.

We can speculate that it may represent what in Shaivism is referred as *sahaja samādhi,* or natural opened-eyed *samādhi.* In *sahaja samādhi,* the liberated being is able to remain fully absorbed in the Self even while going about his or her daily life. The progression from closed-eyed *samādhi* to opened-eyed *samādhi* is stressed within the Kashmir Shaivism tradition, and the antinomian practices within the Kaula school of Shaivism (such as consuming any of the Five Jewels or partaking of the three Ms) were aimed, in part, at allowing the yogin to stabilize his *samādhi* even when not sitting in formal meditation.[95]

In studying all of Patañjali's levels of absorption, nowhere does he explicitly state that the yogin's *samādhi* occurs outside of his closed-eyed meditation practice. But since the final *dharma-megha samādhi* leads to absolute liberation which is permanent and irreversible, logic dictates that it must also apply to the waking state, otherwise it would fall short of being an absolute state.

Five-Step Model and Patañjali

Now that we have looked at Patañjali's levels of meditative absorption, the question remains as to how they align with our five-step model. To review, we established the following five phases of meditation:

95. The three Ms refer to *madya* (wine), *māṃsa* (meat), and *maithuna* (sexual intercourse). In ancient times partaking of wine and meat, as well as sexual intercourse with a lower caste woman, was considered impure and scandalous. Employing them within a ritual setting was designed to break any lingering mental conditioning that causes the yogin to experience that any action or object can exist outside of consciousness. The three Ms were not the only substances or activities involved in Tantric ritual. An even more scandalous set of substances called the Five Jewels composed of bodily fluids and excretions were also employed in Kaula Tantric ritual.

Phase 1:   Settling into our posture, mantra repetition, and focusing attention at the center between each repetition;

Phase 2:   First wave of *kriyās*;

Phase 3:   First Milestone: breaking through the sleep barrier;

Phase 4:   Passage through *tandrā*;

Phase 5:   Second Milestone: yogic death, merging of the breath into the central channel, rise of the Kundalini, *krama mudrā*, and liberation.

Patañjali's stages of *dhāraṇā* and *dhyāna* as well as the first levels of *samādhi* (*savitarka* and *nirvitarka samādhi*) fall within phases one and two of our model. In essence, everything that transpires prior to breaking through the sleep barrier, including merging with the object of contemplation as well as the initial wave of *kriyās*, all unfold prior to or during *savitarka* and *nirvitarka samādhi*. After the body becomes still like a statue and the life energy disengages from the five sense organs, the yogin pierces through the sleep barrier and enters into the *tandrā* state in which our awareness makes direct contact with the subtle elements (*tanmātras*) that make up the senses. Reaching *tandrā* (phases three and four) corresponds to the *Yoga Sūtra's savicāra* and *nirvicāra samādhi*.

It is also worth noting that once we reach the state of *nirvicāra samādhi*, the limit of human willpower is reached and from that point forward it is the direct power of the Self that propels us into the last stages of *samādhi* where our remaining *saṃskāras* are finally destroyed.

Sānanda and *Sasmita* are the next levels of *samādhi* in the *Yoga Sūtra*, and these are located within phase five of our model. After passing through *nirvicāra samādhi*, the breath is sipped down into *sushumnā nāḍī* and the Kundalini flashes forth. From this point on, either we are meditating with the hope that the Kundalini will rise to the highest chakra (if the rise has been partial), or we are gradually stabilizing in *krama mudrā*. Here we enjoy full absorption into the bliss of the causal body or into the I-feeling itself. As meditation progresses through the force of the Self, any remaining *saṃskāras* are burnt away, leading the yogin into *nirbīja samādhi* which then stabilizes into *dharma-megha samādhi*.

Regarding the little understood *dharma-megha samādhi*, I simply equate it with the final opened-eyed *samādhi*, usually referred to as *sahaja samādhi*. Finally, it is important to keep in mind that the correlation between Patañjali's levels of *samādhi* and our five phases of meditation is only meant to serve as a general guide for readers who are academically inclined. If we are able to reach *tandrā* within our lifetime and experience its intense purification, then we will already have achieved an exalted state of yoga.

Other Names for Samādhi

Before ending the discussion on *samādhi*, a quick review of a few alternative names for meditative absorption that we might encounter in our readings is helpful.

In Advaita Vedanta the terms *savikalpa* and *nirvikalpa samādhi* are used: *sa* (with) and *nir* (without) *vikalpa* (conceptualization). *Savikalpa samādhi* can be identified with all the levels of *samprajñāta samādhi*, while *nirvikalpa* with the *nirbīja samādhi* of Patañjali.

Within Kashmir Shaivism, we read of *nimīlana* and *unmīlana samādhi*. *Nimīlana samādhi* covers all phases of closed-eyed *samādhi*. When the yogin is able to extrovert his *samādhi* into opened-eyed unity Awareness (meaning that his identity as pure Awareness persists even when viewing the objective world), that is termed *unmīlana samādhi*.

Unmīlana samādhi can be equated with *sahaja samādhi*, which, as stated above, may be the same as *dharma-megha samādhi*. The point is that different traditions use different names to denote the same inner states.

Sri Ramana, for his part, categorized *samādhi* into three different types:

1. *Savikalpa samādhi*. Here *samādhi* is maintained by the application of constant effort. The moment Self-attention wavers, the yogin is thrown back into the ordinary state of mind where there is a perceiver, perceiving, and an object perceived. This *samādhi* is commensurate with Patañjali's *samprajñāta samādhi* up to the level of *nirvicāra samādhi*.

2. *Kevala nirvikalpa samādhi*. In this state there is a temporary but effortless Self-awareness, but the ego still persists. In this *samādhi* there is no body consciousness and no ability to function in the world. But as soon as the meditation session ends, the ego reappears. This is the same as Patañjali's *sānanda* and *sasmita samādhi*, including *asamprajñāta* and possibly even *nirbīja samādhi*.

3. *Sahaja nirvikalpa samādhi*. This is the final state of opened-eyed *samādhi*, and it is continuous and unbreakable, i.e., it is *dharma-megha samādhi* or simply *sahaja samādhi*.[96]

Final Comments

When faced with so many types of *samādhi*, we can forgive ourselves if we feel disillusioned at the prospect of having to scale what seems like a Mount Everest of meditative absorption. It might feel like an impossible task, so why even bother trying? Yet we would be wise to remember that by the age of five or six, a child already understands that he or she must spend years moving from grade school to high school, and

---

96. Sri Ramana's *samādhi* categories are found in Godman, *Be As You Are*.

further through college or university. The classroom's long arc is not only accepted as a natural and inevitable progression, most kids look forward to advancing through each new level. To their minds, each phase presents an exciting fresh start that is full of promise and adventure.

This, of course, is how we should approach our meditation journey. Moreover, some phases of meditation can be traversed with relative speed. For example, it may only take a few months for some of us to penetrate into *tandrā*, which places us in the *savicāra* level of *samādhi*. Regardless of how many levels of *samādhi* we need to master, the awful alternative would be to not meditate at all, causing us to remain prisoners of the limited body-mind that keeps us restless and unfulfilled. "Feeling of duality is hell," Sri Guru Bhagawan said.[97]

More importantly, we should remember that Patañjali's stages are only one account of the inner realms. All yogic systems should be viewed more as organizational and reference tools than as absolute truths. If, from the onset, we make our I-feeling the target of our attention, our experience of *samādhi* will not proceed as rigidly or systematically as Patañjali indicates. So instead of always wondering where we are, if we follow the broader five-step model set out in this book, then we only need to concern ourselves with one major milestone: penetrating into *tandrā*. We can divide our progress into pre-*tandrā* and post-*tandrā*. Once we manage to enter *tandrā*, we can also view the entire breadth of experience that follows as a single unified phase (until we experience the divine yogic death). In this way, keeping track of levels or phases becomes unnecessary. As Sri Ramana constantly reminds us, from the start, our entire attention should be aimed solely on our I-feeling, meaning that we should not even bother to think about levels or phases.

Finally, no matter how our inner journey unfolds, we can

---

97. *Chidākāsh Gīta,* verse 174.

be motivated by the thought that each stage of yoga has its own inherent rewards. The *Shiva Sūtras* proclaim: *vismayo yogabhūmikāḥ*, "The phases of yoga are filled with wonder."[98] As I like to say, there is nothing worthier, holier, or more sacred than our efforts to still our mind.

98. *Shiva Sūtras*, 1:12.

CHAPTER NINE

The Role of Celibacy in Support of *Samādhi*

If the title of this chapter makes us cringe, it does not mean that we should close the book and throw away our plans to establish a meditation practice. While celibacy has an important place in yoga, clearly the vast majority of us have no interest in its practice. Nevertheless, a frank discussion on the role of celibacy is badly needed, given the current trend to characterize its use in support of meditation as misguided or archaic. With this in mind, the pages below are not intended to discourage, but to educate, and we can breathe easy with the knowledge that a tremendous amount of spiritual growth is possible to achieve without ever submitting to the sacrifices that celibacy entails.

The need for celibacy to attain higher states of awareness has fallen into great discredit over the last fifty years. A century ago, within yogic circles the need to maintain celibacy in the service of meditation was a given. After all, the great Hindu and Buddhist monastic traditions, with their many ashrams and monasteries, were established not only as places ideally suited for study and meditation, but to help aspirants rise above lust. But ever since tantra was introduced to the West, the notion of celibacy as a prerequisite to attain *samādhi* has been pushed to the side. Some of the arguments against strict celibacy are as follows: Since everything is nothing but consciousness, goes the thinking, there should be no need to deprive ourselves of any experience as long as we are able to recognize it as a manifestation of consciousness. Moreover, sexual energy, being a powerful expression of Shakti, can and should be harnessed to help raise the Kundalini. And since the dual energies of Shiva and Shakti are forever trying to unite, if we spiritualize our sexual encounters by infusing them with proper awareness, then we will hasten or aid the evolution of consciousness. After all, the great Master Abhinavagupta himself participated in Tantric sexual rites.[99]

There are numerous problems with the above arguments. To start, we don't drink cyanide, despite knowing that it is nothing but consciousness, for the simple reason that as long as we feel ourselves to be an individual person, then the objects before us are not consciousness at all, but remain objects that can either help or harm us. The ability to rise above restrictions and observances begins *after* we attain Self-awareness, not before. In this way, mere intellectual knowledge that everything is consciousness is not meant as a license to indulge. Book knowledge is but a stepping stone into the disciplines that enable Self-awareness to unfold.

But the question remains: Why should sex, of all possible things, be the one pleasure we have to renounce? It sounds so masochistic, puritan, and dogmatic. And the religious guilt often associated with sexual desire makes the entire enterprise of celibacy seem old fashioned and out of date. Instead, Kashmir Shaivism, with its all-embracing revelation that everything is consciousness, shows a new way that is wiser and more progressive. Or does it?

The first notion to keep in mind is that, in reality, the small group of disciples around Abhinavagupta practiced serious discipline. They were highly ritualistic, following many do's and don'ts, and were not even encouraged to mingle with other yogic groups.[100] Abhinavagupta himself never married

---

99. Kanti Chandra Pandey, *Abhinavagupta: An Historical and Philosophical Study* (Varanasi: Chaukhamba Amarabharati Prakashan, 2006).

100. Alexis Sanderson, "A Commentary on the Opening Verses of the Tantrasāra of Abhinavagupta," in *Sāmarasya: Studies in Indian Arts, Philosophy,*

and most likely remained celibate his entire life outside of the highly controlled Tantric sexual rituals he presided over.[101] Furthermore, those who were allowed to participate in such rites were highly advanced yogins who had already mastered very high levels of closed-eyed *samādhi*. Abhinavagupta said that only one out of a hundred thousand disciples were fit to be initiated into this form of practice.[102] The purpose of those rituals (which included other antinomian practices beyond sexual intercourse such as the consumption of meat and alcohol) was to help highly evolved yogins transition from closed-eyed meditation into a permanent, opened-eyed Awareness. It is only after the *prāna* has been completely purified, the mind completely stilled, and the *sushumnā nāḍī* fully unfolded that the yogin can truly experience the external world of objects and sensations as pure Consciousness. And it is only thereafter that the pleasure and intensity of sexual contact (or any other sensation, for that matter) can be harnessed as an access point into the expanse of pure Awareness. In this light, Kashmir Shaivism is not nearly as "progressive" as some people would like to think.

More than any other sensation, sexual desire (and orgasm in particular) negatively affects our spiritual practice, weakening both body and mind. But the issue is not framed by questions of sin or morality as found in the Judeo-Christian tradition. Instead, the need for celibacy is based on nothing more than straightforward yogic mechanics.

Starting with the body, since the primary goal of meditation is to sever the association of consciousness to the body

and Interreligious Dialogue in Honour of Bettina Bäumer, ed. Sadananda Das and Ernst Fürlinger (New Delhi: D.K. Printworld, 2005).

101. Pandey, *Abhinavagupta.*

102. Alexis Sanderson, "Meaning in Tantric Ritual," in *Essais sur le Rituel III: Colloque du Centenaire de la Section des Sciences religieuses de l'École Pratique des Hautes Études*, Bibliothèque de l'École des Hautes Études, Sciences Religieuses, vol. 102, ed. A.-M. Blondeau and K. Schipper (Louvain-Paris: Peeters, 1995).

and mind, whatever strengthens our identification to the body is by definition counterproductive. As we all know, nothing anchors us more deeply into body awareness than sexual gratification. Sexual urges are by nature a symptom of limited body awareness, for if we are not identified to being a body, sexual desire cannot arise. Yielding to sexual craving greatly strengthens our limited body awareness which then leads to renewed sexual desires. It also agitates the mind, which is the very opposite to the state of meditation. In order to break the cycle, sexual cravings must be controlled for our attention to turn inward and rest in our I-consciousness.

The awareness of being a body that sexual pleasure continually reinforces is not the sole reason to practice celibacy. The mechanics of how spiritual energy accumulates in the body also favors the observance of celibacy. As discussed earlier, when we meditate our body accumulates Shakti, our *nāḍīs* are unblocked, and our *prāṇas* refined. Like a vessel, our body begins to fill with a pulsating white light that can actually be seen in the dark and which signals that the purification of the body is taking place.

The more we meditate, the more Shakti we accumulate, but to hold that Shakti requires a body full of strength and vitality. The process works as follows: from the food we eat, the air we breathe, and the sunlight we are exposed to, we accumulate *prāna*, and a portion of that energy is converted into sexual fluid. Normally, the sexual fluid and its inherent energy are expelled during sexual activity, and the process of rebuilding begins anew as we consume more food, air, and sunlight.

If the sexual fluid is retained, however, it converts into *ojas*, which some consider a form of Shakti, while others consider it to be an actual yellow fluid that accumulates in the bone marrow.[103] As we all know, sexual fluid in both men and women is no ordinary fluid. From a single drop a life is born.

103. Swami Muktananda, *In the Company of a Siddha: Interviews and*

In a man's case, beyond the glandular secretions that make up semen, sexual fluid contains *tejas*, or light, which is composed of heat and vital energy. When accumulated, the *tejas* aspect of sexual fluid is what gets converted into *ojas*. Sri Aurobindo explains that retained *retas* (sexual fluid) progressively refines into *tapas* (heat), to *tejas* (light), to *vidyut* (electricity), and finally into *ojas*.[104] When *ojas* is allowed to accumulate, it spreads throughout the body, filling it with strength, health, and glow, making the yogin shine with the power of *vīryā* (vitality). In this way, the body becomes strong and supple enough to withstand the enormous forces generated by the Shakti during meditation. Specifically, there are phases where the body heats up, and without a strong amount of *ojas* supporting the entire system, the meditative fire will consume the body's juices, causing it to grow weak. Moreover, if *ojas* is lost through orgasm, the Shakti we draw down in meditation is also lost, and neither our body, our subtle *nāḍīs*, nor our *prānas* can undergo their required purifications. In fact, it is only after a great amount of Shakti is accumulated that the sexual current, which normally flows downward, can turn upward, enabling the Kundalini to rise. Accordingly, a proper storehouse of *ojas* is essential to create a platform for the divine Shakti to unfold, and without the latter, the mind has no hope of becoming one-pointed. Put simply, just as a bucket with holes cannot contain water, a body that does not conserve its sexual fluids cannot accumulate Shakti; and this brings all yogic processes to a halt. It also goes without saying that beyond the physiological differences, the process above applies equally to women.

It comes as no surprise that some people do not accept the correlation between sexual abstinence and the body's

---

Conversations with Swami Muktananda (Ganeshpuri: Gurudev Siddha Peeth, 1981).

104. Kishor Gandhi, *Light on Life Problems: Sri Aurobindo's Views on Important Life Problems* (Pondicherry: Sri Aurobindo Ashram, 1987).

vitality. But instead of taking anyone's word on it, we should experiment for ourselves. Generally, after orgasm the mind's cravings quiet down for a period of time, causing a short-lived feeling of peace and satisfaction. But the cravings soon return, and repeated orgasm weakens the body, dulls the mind, and leads to feelings of depression and restlessness.

If the above sounds like old-fashion religious scaremongering, then the reader should experiment with a trial period of celibacy. After only a few months of practice, a deep meditator will come to appreciate the importance of celibacy, not from reading books or listening to sermons but through the direct insight that arises during meditation. In order to verify that indulging in sex is diametrically opposed to Self-realization, we should aim to experience at least six months of celibacy combined with one hour of daily meditation to be able to appreciate the qualitative difference between meditating as a celibate versus meditating as a sexually active person.

If losing our sexual fluids negatively affects the body, the effects on our mind are just as great. Spiritual life demands that we turn our mind inward toward the formless Self, but in the grip of lustful thoughts our mind is externalized to the extreme. We tend to forget about our I-sense, our mantra, the holy scriptures, and our Guru, all because we crave to enjoy a few minutes of contact with another body.

If we examine lust carefully, removing it from its context and looking upon it as energy alone, it becomes apparent that lust is an energy that like any terrible itch demands to be scratched. In other words, lust is a blind energy that only serves itself. It has zero concern or care for the other person who is its object (which is the opposite of love). From this perspective, we can compare lust to a bout of extreme thirst that has to be quenched at all costs. But unlike thirst which has insentient water as its target, with lust the target is another human being, which is what makes it so concerning since it can lead the mind into committing any number of sexual crimes. Moreover, while we need water to survive, the body can live perfectly well without sex.

For these reasons, trying to romanticize lust by suggesting that it is simply Lord Shiva's attempt to unite with his consort Shakti is not helpful. And while from the highest perspective every contact between subject and object can be viewed as "sexual" in the sense that every cognitive transaction is really Shiva embracing Shakti, such poetic renderings of the workings of Consciousness have no positive effect on our *sādhanā*. In fact, they can prove quite detrimental if they dilute or obfuscate our need for self-restraint.

Within the context of ordinary life, sexual urges and sexual enjoyment are perfectly natural, but for the yogin who truly longs to experience the indescribable bliss and peace of liberation, of all the inner obstacles lust is the most difficult to overcome.

Modern seekers become very agitated when they are told that sex is an obstacle to Self-awareness. There is such attachment to sexual pleasure and the escape it offers from the stresses of daily life that the thought of having to restrain the sexual impulse seems overwhelming. After all, if sex is so contrary to spiritual development, why is it that all human beings have an innate sexual impulse?

Spiritual teachers have always been questioned on the relationship between sexual activity and Self-realization. Unlike other negative passions such as greed, selfishness, hatred, jealousy, and so on, overcoming lust presents its own unique challenges because of its enjoyable nature. If we are possessed by a sudden fit of anger or jealousy, we immediately recognize such emotions as negative and we feel relieved when they disappear. But the same cannot be said of lust. When we feel a sexual urge, our instinct is to run toward it instead of away from it.

Because it is counterintuitive to resist an impulse that gives us so much pleasure, saints and sages understand the hardships involved in trying to overcome lust. We never, for example, hear a Guru teach that it is okay to feel a little hatred or a little enmity for our fellow human being. But we do hear them teach that it is not harmful to indulge in disciplined sexual activity, which begs the question of why?

When a Guru teaches that householders (individuals not living in a monastic environment) are permitted to enjoy a regulated amount of sexual activity, devotees misinterpret this to mean that celibacy is not a fundamental requirement to attain Self-realization. After all, we have all been taught that marriage is not an obstacle to spiritual growth. And we all know that lovemaking is an essential part of the social contract of marriage. So while there is no doubt that sex is a fundamental part of marriage, when it comes to our *sādhanā* the essential point is being missed. What is critical from a yogic perspective is to understand that the attainment of *samādhi* can never be achieved without our ability to become established in perfect celibacy. The word *growth* is not the same as the word *samādhi*. Sexually active seekers can still achieve much spiritual growth, but they will not achieve meditative absorption in the true sense of the word. *Tandrā*, for example, can only be reached after we are well established in celibacy. So even though it is perfectly natural for ordinary individuals to enjoy sex, we should consider whether the same rules apply after the pursuit of Self-awareness becomes a central part of our lives.

To answer the question above, spiritual teachers allow for regulated sexual activity simply because perfect celibacy is so incredibly difficult to achieve. We may observe it for short periods of time, stretching out for months or even a few years, but to sustain it indefinitely is extremely difficult. This is even more true in today's world where sexual messaging is all around us and access to sexually explicit content is only a mouse click away. Moreover, celibacy cannot be a forced behavior. The desire to practice celibacy should arise naturally as an offshoot of our meditative contact with the Self. Since only a select number of devotees will have enough spiritual longing to make *sādhanā* their life's priority, for the masses of seekers who are leading family lives and who are engrossed in the world, there is little benefit in stressing a teaching that they do not have the capacity or interest to practice. If the longing for God and the desire for liberation are not firmly rooted in the seeker's heart, there is not much point in discussing the merits of celibacy or renunciation in general.

For couples who are immersed in busy careers and inundated with daily worries, their affections for each other can be an essential part of life. For this reason, it may not be possible for all devotees to practice celibacy, nor would a Guru expect everyone to be celibate. Nonetheless, it is naive to consider that the sexual activity between a husband and wife amounts to a yogic act just because they are devoted to God. When families come to a Guru to receive blessings, the last thing the Guru will do is alienate such devotees by focusing on celibacy. But to those who are fit for true meditative absorption, the Guru will encourage them to be celibate. Otherwise there can be no justification for the division between celibate ashramites and lay devotees. Yet some Tantric teachers make it sound as if the entire tradition of observing *brahmacharya* (celibacy) is unnecessary.

And what about the fact that all humans are born with innate sexual impulses? That we are sexual creatures does not mean that we are condemned to be subservient to our carnal instincts. Within the body there is an expanse of pure Consciousness where the very idea of sex is absent. At our deepest level, lust and other by-products of body identification are nonexistent. In response to the question of how to root out the sex idea, Sri Ramana answered: "By rooting out the false idea of the body being the Self. There is no sex in the Self. Be the Self and then you will have no sex troubles."[105] Sri Bhagawan Nityananda, for his part, said: "Sensual life is

105. Godman, *Be As You Are*.

153

beastly life."[106] As far as I can tell, none of these statements sound like ringing endorsements for sexual activity.

That we experience natural sexual impulses in our current limited state does not mean that we should not strive to transcend them. Although sex is routine for ordinary human beings, the same should not be said for those who embark on a serious meditative journey. Instead of dismissing ourselves as hopelessly sexual, we should strive to develop our spiritual potential by remembering the example set by the lives of the many celibate yogins who have inspired us along the way.

To deny the necessity of being celibate in order to strengthen the body and accumulate Shakti is the same as denying the necessity for a marathon runner to control his or her diet because everyone else is eating whatever they want. Compared to ordinary individuals, Olympic athletes appear as fanatics when it comes to the intense disciplines they keep. Such athletes live highly regulated lives; they get up at the crack of dawn to train for hours and strictly control when and what foods they consume. In addition, for the sake of winning, many athletes abstain from sexual intercourse prior to a competition because they experience firsthand that the loss of energy adversely affects their performance. But how many of us point a finger at them for following such severe disciplines? Instead, we shower them with applause when they step onto the podium to receive their medals.

When it comes to high-level athletes, we accept their extreme forms of discipline because we accept that self-control translates into Olympic level performances. We understand the relationship between diet control, enforced hours of sleep, and intense training with winning an athletic competition. In short, we can rationally connect the dots. But this is not the case with spiritual practice because the process is so subtle and internal. For an outsider who has never experienced devotion,

---

106. *Chidākāsh Gīta,* verse 178.

inner bliss, or stillness of mind, any talk of controlling our natural impulses for the sake of a spiritual goal sounds either dogmatic or downright harmful as they do not understand the mechanics of yoga.

Unfortunately, the same inability to truly understand the process of yoga can persist even for seekers who have spent years on the path. We may experience an inner longing for God or for the grace of an authentic Guru, but we may not understand how it all works. Unless our understanding is transformed as a result of sustained practice, no amount of book reading will sway us because the pull of lust is simply too strong.

As stated above, sex stimulates the outward flow of the mind, strengthens our limited body identification, and dissipates our accumulated spiritual energy. Since our efforts in yoga are designed to reverse these very conditions, we should contemplate the teaching that sexual intercourse is a serious obstacle to Self-realization. That said, we should neither fear nor despise our natural sexuality. Paramhansa Yogananda said:

> If the sexual impulse were taken away from you, you would realize you had lost your greatest friend. You would lose all interest in life. Sex was given to you to make you strong. The more you give in to it, the weaker you become. But when you master it, you'll find that you've become a lion of happiness.[107]

In other words, the same sexual energy that motivates us in life can also move us beyond our humanity and into the divine. In this way sexual energy is a double-edged sword that can project us outward into the chaos of duality or carry us inward

107. J. Donald Walters, Swami Kriyananda, Yogananda (Paramahansa), *Conversations with Yogananda* (Nevada City, CA: Crystal Clarity Publishers, 2004).

into the very center of peace, bliss, and knowledge. The secret of course is how we choose to use our sexual energy: either we conserve it in the service of Self-awareness or we expend it in the service of limited body-mind identification.

For these reasons, we must be careful when we encounter individuals who teach that any form of self-control is an ignorant or inferior approach to *sādhanā*. We should remind such teachers of the monastic traditions that have persisted for thousands of years, or that a close study of the biographies of enlightened beings show that they all practiced celibacy, including the Shaivite masters.

In this light, there comes a time in our *sādhanā* when we realize that to have a real chance at attaining the bliss of the Self, total commitment is necessary. Day by day we pivot our attention away from external objects, keeping it firmly locked on our I-sense. This does not mean that we should all of a sudden stop watching movies, going to restaurants, or doing most of the things we normally enjoy. But if we truly want to be able to still our mind, at some time or another we will have to accept the need to restrain our senses, with particular emphasis on sexual gratification.

Nevertheless, as previously mentioned not every committed meditator who is married or in a relationship should attempt to practice celibacy. When family is involved, careful consideration must be paid to the needs of one's spouse and to the best interests of the family. Generally, families should not be broken apart in the name of yoga, but neither should a yogin be precluded from the opportunity of making significant progress in *sādhanā*. In such situations a compromise to reduce and regulate sexual activity is best, although the mechanics of yoga being what they are, any loss of sexual fluid will impair our meditation regardless of circumstantial considerations.

In the end, full integration between our transcendent and immanent selves will only occur after we plunge deeply into closed-eyed *samādhi*, and not before. If we want to transmute our humanity into divinity, then we must be willing to make the sacrifices it entails, for the inner mechanics of yoga are timeless, eternal, and unaffected by changes in culture or society. In other words, it does not matter if we were meditating five hundred years ago or today, the loss of sexual fluid equates with loss of Shakti, which in turn prevents us from attaining true stillness of mind.

Strategies in Support of Celibacy

If we are to stand a chance at being celibate, we will need the support of several methods. To begin, celibacy should only be attempted by a person who meditates on a daily basis. Otherwise, abstinence can be harmful, since our pent-up sexual energy will have nowhere to go. When we meditate, the Shakti we draw down sublimates the sexual energy into peace, bliss, and one-pointedness of mind. The energy that would normally flow downward and be expressed as lust is consumed in the service of making the mind one-pointed. For this reason, those who practice celibacy without meditating end up injuring themselves or worse (the Catholic Church's sexual abuse scandals come to mind). As long as our mind remains extroverted, there is no possibility for our sexual energy to be used for a higher purpose. Doing so is nothing but repression, and as we shall see, proper control of the sexual impulse is not an act of repression.

Likewise, celibacy should only be attempted if we have strong feelings of devotion for God or Guru. The inner life of a yogin is not as dry and austere as it may appear from the outside. Although a great deal of discipline is followed, inside the yogin feels a deep current of love for his Guru, for the scriptures, and for the ideal of Self-awareness. If, on the other hand, our practice feels mechanical or chore-like, something is missing, and it is very unlikely that we will succeed in abstaining from our natural sexual impulses. As Sri Ramana said:

> It is easy to put on the appearance of *brahmacharya* but to adhere to it to the end is very difficult. It is only fit for courageous and mature people endowed with intense detachment.[108]

Sri Ramakrishna stated as follows:

> After a process of severe struggle with one's lower nature and assiduous practice of spiritual discipline leading to Self-knowledge, one attains the state of *samādhi*. Then the ego with all its train vanishes. But it is very difficult to attain *samādhi*; the ego is very persistent. That is why we are born again and again into this world.[109]

In truth, practicing celibacy is not a decision we make just out of the blue. When we are deeply committed to meditating, the impulse to become celibate arises naturally, since the very act of meditating means focusing on our I-sense and ignoring our body and mind. As we begin to stabilize our contact with the Self, our desire to experience the externalized mind-flow through our five senses diminishes greatly. In this way, the calling to practice celibacy should arise naturally as an off-shoot of a successful meditation practice.

That said, even if we are meditating well, it does not mean that we will suddenly possess full control over our sex drive or that we will no longer feel any sexual desire. No matter how deep our meditation is, we will always have to remain vigilant and work hard to control the sudden upsurges in lust,

---

108. Sadhu Natanananda, David Godman, eds., *Sri Ramana Darsanam: An Explanation of the Truth behind Bhagavan's Life and Teachings* (Tiruvannamalai: Sri Ramanasramam, 2002).
109. Sri Ramakrishna, *Sayings of Sri Ramakrishna*, n.127.

especially since heightened sexual desire itself manifests as an important phase in meditation.[110] In reality lust can never be completely eradicated, for as long as there is even the slightest identification to the body, the sex drive will remain present and disturb us from time to time. Accordingly, we should not wait to feel completely free of lust before we decide to practice celibacy. We have to make a start of it at some point, and in the beginning we will have to endure a certain amount of discomfort as occasional lust is met by yogic resistance. As we can imagine, the first couple of months will be the most difficult since our habituated tendencies will push back against any resistance they encounter.

With this in mind, let us examine a few strategies to help us support our practice. First, we should not think of celibacy as repressing our sex drive. Repression implies bottling up a force without addressing its root cause. It is like trying to stop a firehose by clamping it with a lid instead of shutting off the valve. Instead, celibacy should be understood as the practice of working with and redirecting our sexual energy as opposed to repressing it.

While it is customary to characterize lust in negative terms (in order to understand the harm that comes to us when we lose our sexual fluids), the energy itself behind the feeling of lust should not be seen as negative but as an expression of Shakti that is instrumental in helping us reach *samādhi*. Raw sexual energy, when severed from its association to a human body, is a vibration of consciousness, and when seen as such it can greatly empower our meditation practice. In this light, sexual energy is actually the fuel that powers our meditation.

Once we realize that there is no need to vilify our sexual energy, we can begin to harness it, and we can rely on a number of powerful *dhāraṇās* that we can summon while in the grip of lust, followed by the core practice of turning all

---

110. The accumulation of *ojas* that leads to the purification of the lower chakras occasionally manifests as strong sexual desire.

our attention onto our I-feeling. And just as in the process of learning how to meditate, once we achieve a certain level of proficiency, we will be able to skip the *dhāraṇās* altogether and jump directly into focusing on our I-consciousness, which is always the highest and most direct way of managing any obstacles that relate to the body-mind.

It is important to keep in mind that the *dhāraṇās* presented below are antidotes to help manage lust after it has already manifested, and as such they are unable to eradicate lust from our system. (Only the simultaneous act of identifying with our I-feeling while turning away from the body-mind can eradicate lust.) But as our practice of Self-attention deepens and expands, we will discover that lust begins to disturb us on a more infrequent basis until the desire only presents itself a few times a year.

The six *dhāraṇās* suggested below are not intended to be used at the same time. We can experiment with them until we find the one that works best for us.

First Dhāraṇā: Raising Lust Up Toward the Sahasrāra Chakra

When we feel the presence of sexual desire, we can try to visualize it as an actual energy that can be re-directed upwards into the *sahasrāra* chakra above our head. This practice can be done at any time.

To begin, we take a slow and deep breath. As the air fills our lungs, we try to feel the current of sexual energy in our pelvic area moving upwards through the *sushumnā nāḍī* until it reaches the uppermost chakra, the *sahasrāra*. It is important to understand that the pressure created by our inhalation helps the energy to move up, and with each inhalation we continue to feel our sexual energy moving up and being absorbed into the *sahasrāra* chakra until the desire fades away.

While performing this *dhāraṇā*, we keep our attention fixed on the *sahasrāra* chakra since entering the higher centers naturally lessens our feeling of being a body. Likewise, as the lust energy melts in our *sahasrāra*, we should experience it as a vibration of consciousness and we can allow the force of the energy to bring us full circle into our I-feeling. Associating sexual energy with consciousness is one of the key factors in being able to sublimate it.

Variations to this *dhāranā* include imagining our Guru sitting within the *sahasrāra*, or even imagining him or her sitting before a fire pit in which the sexual energy is being consumed. If we do not have a Guru, we can imagine our sexual energy being fed into the fire pit alone. Alternatively, we can envision a bright full moon in our *sahasrāra* and the sexual energy dripping into a cool pool of water that sits beneath the moon.

After we have gained some control over our sexual desire, the third step is to shift our attention away from our visualization and sink it directly into our I-feeling. If lust returns, we can repeat this or any other *dhāranā*.

Second Dhāranā: Pouring Lust into the Mūlādhāra or Svādhishthāna Chakra

Instead of visualizing our sexual energy pouring into the *sahasrāra* chakra, a similar practice is to feel that our sexual heat is being pulled away from our genitals and guided into our *mūlādhāra* chakra in the perineum area. We can also choose to direct the sexual energy into the *svādhishthāna* chakra below the navel if we find it difficult to conceptualize the location of *mūlādhāra* chakra. After a few minutes of interiorizing our energy in this way, we should bring our attention into our I-feeling.

Third Dhāranā: Equating Lust with the Pleasure of Sex

Another effective approach is to close our eyes and pay very close attention to the vibration of the sexual energy that has taken over our body. When examined closely, sexual energy is equal part irritant (because it makes us crave something we lack) and equal part pleasure. Lust has its own inherent pleasure, since it is the first stage of a sensation that terminates in orgasm. Like a seed that contains a tree, lust already contains within it the anticipated pleasure of sex; if we stop thinking about the physical object of lust or the sex act and immerse ourselves directly in the pure energy of lust, we will discover that lust itself is highly pleasurable. In fact, the craving for sexual contact is easily eliminated the moment we conflate lust with the pleasure of actual sexual intercourse. Put differently, by equating lust with the pleasure of intercourse, we discover that they are very similar, which helps reduce the craving for another body. Accordingly, during the height of lust we should try to feel that we are already enjoying the ecstasy of sexual union and then we should try to associate that pleasure with the abstract bliss of pure Consciousness. After a few minutes, we should try to feel that we have entered the period of calm that follows orgasm. When done properly, this *dhāraṇā* allows us to quickly absorb sexual desire while at the same time conserving our vital fluids.

Fourth Dhāraṇā: Converting Sexual Energy into Pure Consciousness

This *dhāraṇā* can be practiced alone or as a continuation of the previous one. After equating lust with sexual pleasure, we are only a step away from experiencing it as a vibration of pure Shakti, and the moment we do so, we are able to devour or digest it completely into Consciousness.

In this *dhāraṇā*, after getting a handle on the sexual desire by equating it with pleasure we are seeking, we take it a step further by equating the feeling of pleasure to the Consciousness that is unrelated to the body but one and the same as our I-feeling. Put differently, we unite sexual energy to our I-feeling. Once we are able to transmute our sexual energy into the experience of pure Consciousness, we no longer see it as a threat to our meditation but as a great fuel that allows our mind to grow extremely one-pointed. If we can try to experience the raw energy of lust as pure Shakti, telling ourselves that it is nothing but fuel for our meditation, our bodies will become filled with *ojas* and over time we will meditate with great power. Moreover, we will no longer fear lust each time it flares up but look to it as an opportunity to create intense yogic heat and purification for our body.

Fifth Dhāraṇā: Dissolving the Object of Lust

If lust is triggered by attraction to a particular individual, we can try to neutralize the desire for another person by subsuming that person into our field of consciousness. The first step in this *dhāraṇā* is to locate our I-feeling, telling ourselves that pure Awareness is what we truly are. Then we expand that Awareness outward to envelop everything around us, with particular emphasis on the person causing our feelings of lust. We visualize that the person is a projection of our own consciousness, meaning that the person is fully contained within our own consciousness. We try to arrive at the understanding or intuition that both our body and the body of the person in question are manifesting within a unified field of consciousness, which means that we already fully possess the person we are lusting over. The feeling of absorbing or dissolving our object of lust (or any object) into our own consciousness can quickly pacify the nagging desire to have contact with a particular person or object. Burning everything into sameness is a primary Tantric practice.

Sixth Dhāraṇā: Visualizing a Sexual Consort

If we are still troubled by the desire to have contact with another body despite all our efforts to merge lust into pure Consciousness, we can practice uniting with a mental consort.

Sitting in our regular meditation posture, we close our eyes and visualize a consort sitting on our lap with her legs wrapped around us in a sexual embrace, or vice versa in the case of a woman. Sexual union with a mental consort allows us to completely melt the feeling of lust into pure bliss and non-dual Awareness. Yet, to ensure the contemplation does not degenerate into an ordinary act of sexual imagination, a few key points should be kept in mind.

First, it is important that the sexual embrace be held in absolute stillness. Like two statues sitting nose to nose, the sexual embrace focuses entirely on melting the sexual energy into the bliss of pure Consciousness, and not on any kind of sexual friction between two bodies.

Since no sexual movement is allowed, we might wonder why we should even bother to visualize a sexual consort. When male and female energies unite, it accelerates our ability to transform lust into meditative bliss. By imagining that we are embracing a consort of the opposite sex, the union of polar opposite energies brings harmony to our mind and pacifies lust's target. But unlike actual union with a real consort, which only highly perfected yogins are allowed to practice, union with a mental consort is much safer. I cannot stress enough that union with a mental consort is not a visualization of having sex. On the contrary, union with a mental consort has little to do with sex and everything to do with calming the mind and transmuting sexual energy into blissful consciousness.

Second, when sitting in mental union, we must synchronize our breathing so that we and our imagined consort are both breathing together in a steady and natural pace. Our inhalation should coincide with our consort's exhalation, and vice versa. Finally, we should try to feel our sexual energy expanding into a formless pulsation of bliss that fills both yogin and consort until both bodies dissolve into pure Being and all traces of lust have disappeared, leaving us completely absorbed in our I-feeling. For the *dhāraṇā* to work, it is important to connect bliss to our I-feeling, recognizing them as one and the same.

Needless to say, visualizing a consort can only be practiced if we happen to be at home or in a quiet place when disturbed by lust. I also do not recommend visualizing a consort until we have gained a high degree of proficiency with the other *dhāraṇās* and have actually experienced the feeling of converting lust into blissful energy.

Further Observations on Celibacy

All of the above *dhāraṇās* are only stop-gap measures designed to allow us to manage lust after it has already taken hold of us. As such, they are not intended as long-term solutions. Instead, to truly sublimate our sex drive is to gradually reduce flare-ups altogether, and the latter is only accomplished through the persistent practice of focusing on our I-feeling and ignoring our body and mind as much as possible. Except for the fifth *dhāraṇā*, we work directly with the energy of lust, never dwelling or engaging with the thoughts that caused lust to arise in the first place.

We must remember that thought is the root cause of lust, and when we cut down a lustful thought even before it is fully formed, choosing instead to revert our attention back onto our I-consciousness, we are engaged in the highest form of yogic austerity. Sadhu Om puts it as follows:

> Aspirants who, in order to destroy evil thoughts like lust, anger and so on, fight against them and thereby think about them fail in their attempts, while aspirants practicing Self-enquiry, who pay their full attention to Self with an indifference toward their thoughts, bypass them easily.[111]

It is a well-known truism that the mind takes on the shape

111. Sri Sadhu Om, *Path of Sri Ramana.*

and color of whatever it dwells on. Like a line carved onto cement, the more our mind dwells on lustful thoughts, the more it is molded by them. In order to disengage the mind from the pull of desire, we should first observe lust as it arises, telling ourselves that we are not the desire. After establishing a gap between our identity and lust, we will find it easier to turn our attention away from lust and onto our I-feeling. By repeatedly keeping our attention fixed on our I-feeling, our mind will grow increasingly subtle, to the extent that the canvass of our mind will transform from cement, to clay, to sand, to water, until all lines of desire disappear as quickly as they arrive. In this way, turning away from sexual thoughts and keeping our attention on our I-feeling is the real master key that grants final success in celibacy. Sri Ramana has said:

> The only way to overcome obstructions to your meditation is to forbid the mind to dwell on them and to introvert it into the Self and there witness unconcernedly all that happens; there is no other method.[112]

If we are disturbed by lust but manage to control it through the combined use of *dhāraṇās* and strong attention to our I-sense, we will soon enter into a deep calm and peace that is similar to what we experience after orgasm but without any of the corresponding loss or weakness. On the contrary, our body will vibrate with great energy and we will feel the positive effects as soon as we sit down for our next meditation session.

As mentioned, the contemplations above are designed to combat lust in the heat of the moment, but there are also secondary, preventive techniques that we can practice when lust is dormant. Since much has already been written about them, the comments below will be brief.

---

112. Arthur Osborne, ed., *The Collected Works Of Ramana Maharshi* (York Beach, ME: Red Wheel / Weiser, 1997).

To begin, we can de-sexualize the human body by imagining it in less than flattering ways. These include visualizing the body stripped of its skin, remembering that only feces, urine, and foul gas are emitted from the pelvic area, remembering that the body stinks if not washed after only a day or two, and so on. A caution here is that only yogins with clear minds should practice such exercises because it is vital not to lose our sense of love and compassion for ourselves and our fellow human beings. Making the body ugly in the mind of a yogin is only designed to de-sexualize it and should not affect the respect, care, and attention we show it, given the fact that the body is a temple of Consciousness.

Other secondary methods include controlling our diet. A vegan diet free of eggs, dairy, and meats is very helpful. Some go as far as banishing onions and garlic, but in my view, if we are counting on dietary restrictions to control lust, then the battle has already been lost. Dietary restrictions (outside of the consumption of meat) will only have modest effects in our ability to remain celibate, though when suffering through a period of increased lust we can try limiting our sleep and reducing our food by a small amount, since too much food and too much sleep aggravate sexual desire. Taking cold showers can also help, but it is not practical to jump into cold water each time we are faced with sexual desire.

Exercising the body when lust presents itself can also serve as a great mitigating strategy, the idea being to distract the body and mind from the pull of lust. On this note Sri Annamalai Swami tells a humorous story: Once, when he was perturbed by the sight of an attractive woman, Sri Ramana ordered him to stand on a large rock that was burning hot under the midday sun, causing great pain to his feet. The shift of attention from the woman's body to his burning feet was enough to dissipate his lustful thoughts.[113] On a second occasion, Sri Ramana instructed Sri Annamalai as follows:

113. Godman, *Living by the Words of Bhagavan.*

Why should you always be thinking that an evil thought occurred at such and such a time in the past? If you instead meditate "to whom does this thought come?" it will fly away of its own accord. You are not the body or the mind, you are the Self. Meditate on this and all your desires will leave you.[114]

All things considered, we should understand that the real force of practice comes from our commitment to meditate daily and from our ability to remain focused on our I-feeling throughout the day. Simply sitting crossed-legged for an hour in and of itself greatly aids in the regulation of lust. Mantra repetition and remembering our Guru are also very helpful in keeping our hearts tender with love for our *sādhanā*, which is a prerequisite for the successful control of sexual desire.

Another important issue, at least as it concerns men, is how to manage the problem of night emissions. The first thing to note is that no matter how dedicated we are, night emissions are not only inevitable, they will probably last for years. It is only after we have established deep contact with the Self that night emissions will diminish in frequency (usually beginning a year into practice).

Because we do not have control of our dreams, the age-old *vāsanas* of past sexual conduct will manifest as sexual dreams. When we experience a night emission, we should not allow feelings of guilt or unworthiness to taint us since such events are beyond our control. Moreover, every now and then the body will create a night emission in order to clear the ejaculatory ducts. Accordingly, the proper way to deal with wet dreams is to ignore them completely and carry on with our practice as if nothing at all has happened. We should never feel that our celibacy has been compromised or that we somehow failed because we experienced a night emission.

114. Ibid.

Final Comments

Even if we are inspired to practice celibacy after committing to a daily meditation practice, the difficult truth is that few of us will be able to sustain complete abstinence for long periods of time. Falling off the horse is inevitable until we have purified our mind and body to a great degree. The latter implies that a certain amount of stillness of mind can definitely be reached without celibacy, but to really dive into the depths of meditation requires a systematic gathering and conserving of all our energies.

Although we may yield to sexual temptation again and again, over time our growing capacity to remain absorbed in our I-feeling will gradually reduce the instances when sexual craving takes us by surprise. The point is that we should not become discouraged if we fail on multiple occasions. It should not be forgotten that sexual gratification is an easy pleasure to experience while the peace and bliss of a quiet mind require some effort to achieve. Therefore, we should not be surprised if we find ourselves swept away by lust from time to time, but instead of feeling defeated, we should feel tremendous compassion for ourselves—compassion that is not tainted by the slightest trace of guilt. Instead, we should pick ourselves up and renew our intention to attain *samādhi*. Even though perfect celibacy is extremely difficult to achieve, we must, above all, remember that the Guru's grace never abandons a sincere devotee, and that the same opportunity to become a great yogin remains just as before we yielded to temptation.

In this light, we should always carry forward as if there was no break in our resolve, since there is nothing more dangerous to a yogin than to feel unworthy. In our efforts we should remember that, before they attained Self-awareness, all great beings had to pass through similar hardships and disappointments. It is only because they did not give up that they became the pure beings we adore today. If other yogins were able to succeed, there is no reason for us not to. Certainly the Guru wishes for us to continue with our practices no matter how many times we fall short of our own noble standards. If we are meant for it, in time the Guru's grace will ensure that complete celibacy is attained.

Finally, it is equally important to remember that if we do not feel capable or inclined to practice celibacy, it does not mean that we should give up our efforts to meditate or focus on our I-feeling. As long as we nurture our practice, we are bound to progress and attain spiritual growth, not to mention the deep relaxation and peace of mind that come to those who practice even a little meditation.

As mentioned in this chapter's opening paragraph, the encouragement to practice celibacy is meant to educate and inspire those few aspirants who are truly ready to make a serious effort toward complete stillness of mind. As to the rest of us, who make up the majority, we would be remiss to deprive ourselves of the absolute joy and stability of mind that a life of meditation provides, no matter how much we enjoy our senses. As our meditation deepens over time, our interests will naturally shift away from the senses, so it would be a mistake to think that our desire to enjoy sex or anything else that life has to offer should disqualify us from taking those crucial first steps toward Self-awareness. Everything will align and fall into place exactly when it is meant to; our sole duty is to maintain our commitment to daily practice.

CHAPTER TEN

Yoga Means Change

For many of us, our *sādhanā* will not be limited to meditating and focusing on our I-feeling. To remain inspired, we can support our practice by reading the words of enlightened sages, studying the scriptures, waving incense daily before a picture of our Guru or a saint we feel connected to, or joining a chanting group. We should also try to spend a few weeks every year in an ashram or retreat where we can immerse ourselves more fully in meditation.

As our meditation grows stronger, we may find that our entire life begins to arrange itself more and more around our practice. And this, of course, invites lots of changes to our external life.

Many beginners who come to yoga do so in the belief that no part of their external life needs to change. After all, meditation is the pursuit of inner consciousness. Gurus themselves repeatedly teach that there is no need to renounce family or city life, that inner renunciation is the true renunciation, and that nothing but our outlook needs to change. Everything is *sādhanā*, goes the teaching.

In truth, such teachings are meant to assuage beginners and encourage them to keep moving toward spiritual practice. No one, after all, likes sudden change. Yet, if we think about, it does not take much to realize how a serious meditation practice will lead to enormous changes in our external life.

First, effective meditation requires that we sit for an hour in the early morning, keeping to the same time. This means that we will have to go to bed at a reasonable hour, which in and of itself affects our lifestyle by cutting into the time we are able to spend with our spouse, children, and friends. Second, effective meditation requires that we abstain from harmful substances such as alcohol and nicotine. Now while smoking is no longer socially acceptable in the way it used to be, drinking alcohol remains an ingrained part of gatherings and business meetings. If we abstain completely from alcohol, business associates or dinner friends may judge us for refusing to have even a sip of wine or beer. And needless to say, any attempt to reduce sexual relations will create instant waves.

As our mind becomes more attracted to the bliss of inner stillness, we may notice deep changes in our personality as well. Some of our old interests may die off. We may stop cursing or being sarcastic, or we may lose interest in listening to certain types of music, watching certain shows, or going to bars or clubs. In short, our social behaviors may shrink as our mind moves away from chasing after external pleasures.

As long as we are alone, there is little consequence, but if we have a family, an active social life, or are in a profession that puts us face to face with other people in social situations, our yogic tendencies will not go unnoticed. And while we might like to believe that in a free world our personal choices should not attract any judgments, in my own experience nothing could be further from the truth.

If we look at the lives of advanced yogins and saints, we do not find them going to restaurants, attending the theater, dancing in clubs, or even spending a week in the Caribbean soaking up the sun. They tend to live in relative isolation, as Swami Lakshmanjoo did, or if they are householders like Sri Nisargadatta, they live highly regulated lives. So the idea that our journey into meditation is strictly internal is somewhat naive. Sri Nisargadatta hinted at this when he spoke as follows:

Stop, look, investigate, ask the right questions, come to the right conclusions and have the courage to act on

them and see what happens. The first steps may bring
the roof down on your head, but soon the commotion
will clear and there will be peace and joy.[115]

The point being made is that we should be prepared to manage, to the best of our ability, the many changes that a meditative life brings about. From a yogic perspective such changes
are highly desirable and essential if we are to have the opportunity to attain Self-awareness. Some of these changes will
manifest without much incidence, while others will lead to
the loss of friendships, jobs, or even significant relationships.
If we are going to shed our limited identity, we will have to
be courageous in the face of criticism and remain steadfast
to our goal. And if we still doubt that a life of meditation is
not exactly compatible with a standard social life, we need
only turn to the example of Sri Muruganar, who left his own
wife to live with Sri Ramana. Although his case is extreme,
what matters is not that Sri Muruganar left his wife, which
any person can do, but that Sri Ramana accepted him into
the ashram without turning him back. This fact should not
be overlooked, especially since there are several quotes by
Sri Ramana where he encourages seekers to continue to live
as householders. Swami Natanananda, one of Sri Ramana's
leading disciples, was of the view that Sri Ramana gave such
advice to people he knew were unfit for a life of self-control,
meaning that such people were not capable of attaining
samādhi in this lifetime.[116] Swami Natanananda's conclusion
is again especially important, because when we walk away
from a saint who instructs us to continue with our regular
householder life (that is, without restraining our senses or
practicing celibacy), we may fall under the wrong impression

---

115. Maurice Frydman, trans., Sudhakar S. Dikshit, ed., *I Am That: Talks
with Sri Nisargadatta Maharaj* (Durham, NC: Acorn Press, 1988).
116. Sadhu Natanananda and Godman, *Sri Ramana Darsanam; Ātma Gīta,*
verses 79–87.

that the saint is telling us we can attain full enlightenment while still carrying on as usual. In fact, all the saint is telling us is that at the moment we are not spiritually mature enough to attain *samādhi*, but to continue moving forward until we develop more interest in the Self and a greater capacity for dispassion. Similarly, Sri Ramakrishna was well known for presenting one view of *sādhanā* to his lay devotees while presenting quite a different one to his renunciate swamis. For his part, Sri Annamalai was very forthcoming when asked by a couple if celibacy was necessary for Self-realization. He said:

> Help each other on the path as friends. If there is any sexual desire you will lose some spiritual power. Even if you just look at someone and feel some desire toward them, you lose a little spiritual energy. In a family situation there are always strong attachments. The husband will give a lot of love to his wife and vice versa. Both will give a lot of love to the children. If you are serious about *sādhanā*, remain unmarried and put all your energy into Self-enquiry. You cannot hold onto the Self while you still have strong attachments to other people.[117]

In light of the above, those who are not ready for true stillness of mind will be presented with a view of *sādhanā* where all their patterns of behavior can remain the same or where only minor adjustments are required, while those who are committed to serious meditation will quickly experience for themselves how fast things actually change. What matters, of course, is that eagerness to observe self-restraint emerges naturally from within, as a fruit of deep practice, and is not artificially imposed by the ego as a form of spiritual posturing.

If practicing celibacy is so important, is it not best to move into an ashram where we can seek shelter from our highly sexualized society? While I do support spending a few weeks

---

117. Godman, *Living by the Words of Bhagavan*.

at an ashram once or twice a year, sadly many ashrams have fallen prey to materialistic concerns that are anything but spiritual, which makes moving in as a long-term resident a possible detriment to our *sādhanā*. Even the ashrams of the great Vishnu Tirth Maharaj have not been spared. When I had the enormous privilege of visiting the realized Master Sri Devendra Vijgyani Maharaj at his home in Rishikesh, he told me that spending time at Vishnu Tirth's ashram in Rishikesh was probably not a good idea since it and many other ashrams remain ashrams in name only. When I asked why, he said that they are being run by ordinary individuals who are no longer motivated or guided by the highest spiritual ideals.

Accordingly, we should be careful before moving into an ashram for an extended period of time unless there is a truly bona fide Self-realized being present in the ashram or we are certain the people running the ashram are honest and sincere. But since locating and identifying an authentically realized Guru is no easy task, it is probably best to undertake our *sādhanā* from home.

In fact, it is a real shame that so many Hindu ashrams have fallen into disrepute, and on this note we should look toward the Buddhist traditions which have done a much better job of nurturing and protecting their monastic environments. This is not to suggest that all Hindu ashrams lack integrity, or that no Buddhist monasteries have fallen prey to corruption, only that we will have to work harder to locate authentic ashrams that still live up to their spiritual ideals.

Conclusion

A lifelong commitment to meditation infuses our life with meaning and purpose, as well as revealing our highest potential as human beings. When we embrace the possibility that we are something more than this mere body and mind, we have taken our first step toward the attainment of supreme Consciousness.

No matter from what angle we approach spiritual life, attaining a higher state of awareness requires that we still our thought waves, and no method is better than to keep our attention fixed on our I-sense. Even a central Tantric text such as the *Pratyabhijñāhṛdayam* teaches that banishing thoughts and watching our I-feeling is a principal method of attainment.[118]

As we move through this great adventure called life, we may find that from time to time our interest and focus on our meditation practice waxes and wanes. There will be periods of effortless commitment where getting out of bed before dawn seems natural and easy, followed by rough patches where all interest in meditation seems to evaporate. Such back and forth occurs naturally due to the mind's contact with the shifting *gunas*, and what matters is being able to find a middle ground between pushing too hard (to the point where we become rigid and unresponsive) and letting ourselves go (to the point where no actual *sādhanā* is being practiced).

As much as possible, we should continue to sit and meditate on a daily basis, knowing that our lack of enthusiasm is but a passing phase. In time, we will catch a second wind and soar once again into the bliss and peace of an almost effortless meditation. If we can stick to our practice through all our perceived ups and downs, we will periodically look over our shoulder and appreciate the enormous fruits our steadfastness has yielded. As we strive in our *sādhanā*, it helps to remember that much of our progress happens beyond the mind's conscious awareness, while at other times entry into states of bliss, peace, or even into *tandrā* are delightfully evident.

In order to be able to meditate for a lifetime, we must embrace meditation as something done for its own sake. Of the many spiritual practices available to us, Self-attention, formal meditation, and mantra repetition are extremely important, as well as developing a deep current of love and devotion for

118. *Pratyabhijñāhṛdayam,* sutra 18.

God or Guru. As long as we make a firm resolve to remain connected to the current of grace that flows unceasingly from our own I-feeling, there is no doubt that the great Self will be attained. As Sri Ramana sings:

> Without knowing Self, what is the use if one knows anything else? If one has known Self, then what else is there to know? When that Self, which shines without difference (as "I am") in all the many living beings is known in oneself, the light of Self will flash forth within one self (as "I am That I am"). This experience of the Self is the shining forth of Grace, the destruction of the "I" (the ego), and the blossoming of bliss. Therefore, so very easy is the science of Self! Ah! So very easy![119]

With folded hands I humbly offer these words to my own Sri Gurudev:

> *Om Namo Bhagavate Nityānandāya. Srī Gurudeva-caraṇārpaṇamastu.*

---

119. Sri Ramana quoted in Sadhu Om, *Sri Ramanopadesa Noonmalai.*

APPENDIX ONE

Meditation Instructions: Repeating Mantra as a Direct Means of Attainment

In the instructions below, we approach mantra as a direct instrument of attainment. Here we make an effort to fully unite with the mantra, giving rise first to the understanding and later to the experience that there is no difference between us, the mantra, and pure Consciousness. In fact, as we lovingly repeat the mantra, we become completely absorbed in its vibration, moving gradually but steadily toward the experience that the entire universe is nothing but the silent vibration of mantra, and that in fact nothing other than its pulsation exists.

Sitting comfortably, close your eyes and gently roll back the shoulders and lift the chin, elongating the back. The neck is soft and relaxed, as are your eyes and jaw.

Place your hands on your knees in *chin mudrā*, palms down with the thumbs touching the forefingers.

Now bring your attention to your breath. Slowly, breathe in deep and exhale long, repeating the process three or four times, each time feeling that the lungs are expanding and are able to carry more air. Continue this slow and deep breathing until your feel that your lungs are nice and open.

Now take a slow and deep inhalation and lower your chin until it almost touches the notch at the base of the neck. Hold the breath for three seconds and then lift the chin, slowly exhaling. Here, both inhaling and exhaling are done through the nostrils. The mouth stays closed with the tip of the tongue resting at the top of the palate.

Breathe in again and repeat lowering the chin and holding the breath for three seconds. Doing so greatly helps to induce stillness of mind.

Raise your chin, allowing the breath to return to normal.

As you breathe normally (no longer lowering your chin), begin to silently repeat the supremely auspicious and grace bestowing mantra *Om Namaḥ Shivāya*, synchronizing each repetition with the incoming and outgoing breath. *Om Namaḥ Shivāya* on the inbreath and *Om Namaḥ Shivāya* on the outbreath.

Allow the attention to slowly move away from the breath and to unite with the sound and vibration of *Om Namaḥ Shivāya*. Feel that your sense of being is completely united to the vibration of *Om Namaḥ Shivāya*. Allow your body, mind, and the external world to melt away. Try to experience that the division between you and the mantra no longer exists. The awareness that witnesses the mantra is the mantra itself. Only the mantra exists, and the entire universe is contained within that vibration. Nothing but *Om Namaḥ Shivāya* exists.

Do not focus too strongly on the syllables. Experience the mantra as a continuous vibration of sound.

If other thoughts arise, do not fight them. Acknowledge them as vibrations of consciousness and return your attention to your I-feeling, while continuing to repeat the mantra. Allow yourself to become completely enveloped by *Om Namaḥ Shivāya*.

Meditate with great love.

APPENDIX TWO

Meditation Instructions: Using the Mantra as Rails to Guide Us into Self-Awareness

In the instructions below, we take the support of mantra to help keep our attention absorbed in our pure I-feeling. Instead of trying to unite with the mantra, we allow the vibration of the mantra to reverberate in the background, both as a way to keep other thoughts at bay and to allow its vibrations to help still the mind. Synchronizing the mantra with the breath and tracing each inhalation to its resting place allows us to repeatedly locate our pure I-sense. In this way, the mantra acts as rails that anchor us in the formless expanse of blissful awareness that is our great Self.

Sitting comfortably, close your eyes and gently roll back the shoulders and lift the chin, elongating the back. The neck is soft and relaxed, as are your eyes and jaw.

Place your hands on your knees in *chin mudrā*, palms down with the thumbs touching the forefingers.

Now bring your attention to your breath. Slowly, breathe in deep and exhale long, repeating the process three or four times, each time feeling that the lungs are expanding and are able to carry more air. Continue this slow and deep breathing until your feel that your lungs are nice and open.

Now take a slow and deep inhalation and lower your chin until it almost touches the notch at the base of the neck. Hold the breath for three seconds and then lift the chin, slowly exhaling. Here, both inhaling and exhaling are done through the nostrils. The mouth stays closed with the tip of the tongue resting at the top of the palate.

Breathe in again and repeat lowering the chin and holding the breath for three seconds. Doing so greatly helps to induce stillness of mind.

Raise your chin, allowing the breath to return to normal.

As you breathe normally (no longer lowering your chin), begin to silently repeat the supremely auspicious and grace bestowing mantra *Om Namaḥ Shivāya*, synchronizing each repetition with the incoming and outgoing breath. *Om Namaḥ Shivāya* on the inbreath and *Om Namaḥ Shivāya* on the outbreath.

Allow your attention to trace the mantra to the silent source at the end of each inhalation, and hold your attention in the space which is the source of both the breath and the mantra. Gradually allow the vibration of the mantra to fade into the background as you hold your attention on your pure I-feeling, your presence of being.

If other thoughts arise, do not fight them. Acknowledge them as vibrations of consciousness and return your attention to your I-feeling, while continuing to repeat the mantra.

As you settle into the stillness at the center of the breath, begin to experience that everything is dissolving into that empty space. Feel that your mind, your body, and the room you are sitting in are dissolving into that empty space. Even the feeling of watching your I-sense begins to disappear, so that only pure Awareness rests in pure Awareness. Feel that the entire universe is absorbed into your I-feeling until nothing else exists. There is perfect oneness, perfect stillness, perfect peace.

Meditate with great love.

ACKNOWLEDGMENTS

Like many others of my generation, my meditative life began on the day I set eyes on that old but classic book: *Autobiography of a Yogi*, by Paramhansa Yogananda. As I became lost in its pages, I felt that its teachings were like precious lost memories rushing back to the surface of my mind. Beyond the book's wisdom, I felt much devotion for Yoganandaji, and my twenty-year-old mind began to burn with the desire to meet an authentic Guru of my own who could guide me through all those wonderful and miraculous yogic adventures.

Not long after, I found myself sitting next to my mother as we zoomed down New York Interstate 87 on our way to a well-known ashram nestled in the snowy Catskill mountains. The year was 1991.

Over the next few days, I soaked it all up: the rising before dawn to meditate, the glorious chanting of devotional hymns and sacred scriptures, and the practice of selfless service. But when I stood before a large black and white picture of Sri Bhagawan Nityananda, my eyes opened wide, and I felt an intense pang of love explode in my chest.

For the divine and incomparable blessing of having Sri Bhagawan in my life, I thank my mother, with whom I had the joy of sharing many more trips to South Fallsburg. For the ashram itself and all the traditional learning and education I received, I bow deeply to Gurumayi Chidvilasananda, who also blessed me with initiation into several mantras that set fire to my meditation.

I also bow deeply to Sri Ramana Maharshi, the divine embodiment of pure Knowledge who destroys spiritual ignorance, stills the mind, and is a great force in my yoga *sādhanā*.

There are other sages that have served as beacons of light: Sri Swami Lakshmanjoo, Sri Nisargadatta Maharaj, Sri Neem Karoli Baba, Sri Annamalai Swami, and Sri Sadhu Om, to name a few. I place my forehead at their holy feet.

In addition to the divine Gurus, I cannot forget the teachers and mentors who have been vital to my spiritual development: Markji (Dr. Mark Dyczkowski), the lion of Tantra who openly receives everyone at his home in Varanasi with so much grace, patience, and humility. Dr. Paul Muller-Ortega, Carlos Pomeda, Sally Kempton, David Godman, and Michael James. We are lucky to have them among us.

I thank my spiritual brothers and sisters in yoga: Rajiv Iyer, Deepa Iyer, Christian Medved, Michael Medved, Tamara Cohen, Jennifer Fisher, Jim Drobnick, Tom Pokinko, Viveka Sankalpa, and Jorge (Narayana) Espinoza. You are my spiritual family.

I mention everyone above because each of them, in their own way, has contributed to the existence of this book.

I am grateful to my brilliant editors: Betsy Robinson and Susan Matheson, whose incredible talents did wonders for the text. To Brandi Doane McCann for her beautiful cover, to Sandra K. Williams for her elegant interior design and ebook production, and to Carol Roberts for compiling the index. To all of you, I owe a sincere debt of gratitude.

Finally, I must return to my beloved Guru, Sri Bhagawan Nityananda of Ganeshpuri, who is none other than Lord Shiva incarnate. May I be blessed with the supreme fortune to always utter your name and remember your form.

Om Namo Bhagavate Nityānandāya! Tasmai Srīgurave Namaḥ.

GLOSSARY

Abhaya mudrā (lit., *gesture of fearlessness*) A physical hand gesture where the right hand is raised, shoulder height, palm facing outward.

Advaita Vedanta (lit., *non-dual end of the Vedas*) An important school of thought in the tradition of non-duality, which stresses the underlying unity between the soul and pure Consciousness, along with the appearance of *māyā*, or illusion, which is responsible for the apparent division between subjects and objects.

Ahankāra The aspect of the mind responsible for causing us to identify with objects of perception such as our thoughts and our body, i.e., the ego. The *ahankāra* maintains our self-identification as a limited individual.

Ājñā chakra (lit., *command center*) The spiritual plexus located between the eyebrows. The *ājñā* chakra is an important point of focus for meditators, as well as the seat of the eight major supranormal powers which activate once the Kundalini Shakti pierces it after rising from the base of the spine.

Anjali mudrā (lit., *gesture of reverence*) A physical hand gesture where the palms of both hands are raised to the heart level and pressed together.

Anuttara Trika (lit., *supreme trinity*) Anuttara refers to the supreme principal of Awareness, the underlying reality. The word *trika*, meaning trinity, references the three principles of *Shiva-Shakti-Nara* or the three supreme energies of *Parā-Parāparā-Aparā* which are fundamental concepts within Kashmir Shaivism. Together, Anuttara Trika is a more precise way to describe the Tantric philosophy more commonly known as Kashmir Shaivism.

Apāna (lit., *inhalation*) One of the five types of *prāna* that moves downward and is responsible for the elimination and excretory functions of the body.

Ardha padmāsana (lit., *half-lotus posture*) A sitting, cross-legged posture where the left foot rests on the floor tucked in close to the right thigh and the right foot is placed over the left thigh. Half-lotus is much easier to hold than full-lotus (both feet resting on opposite thighs) and is supportive of very deep and long meditation sessions.

Asamprajñāta samādhi An extremely advanced level of meditative absorption where the mind is devoid of any objects of contemplation but is still filled with latent mental impressions that serve to veil the intellect from the direct awareness of pure Consciousness.

Āsana (lit., *seat*) A physical posture adopted by meditators that allows for comfortable sitting with a straight spine for extended periods of time; a small woolen cloth used to shield the meditator's body from the earth beneath it.

Ātmā-nishta (lit., *Self-abidance*) A term used to describe the final state of permanent absorption in pure Consciousness.

Ātmā-vicāra (lit., *Self-enquiry*) The name of the principal practice taught by Sri Ramana Maharshi, where one's attention is directed inward onto itself. In *ātmā-vicāra* we repeatedly attempt, through gentle effort, to remain aware of our felt-presence, the bare feeling that we exist apart from the body and mind. Proper Self-inquiry is only possible after we have intellectually accepted that Consciousness precedes matter, and not vice versa. Posing a question to ourselves such as "Who am I?" or "Who is the thinker?" can help the intellect identify with the innate Awareness.

Ātman The pure inner Consciousness devoid of any associations with any objects or adjuncts, both gross or subtle. The ground of pure Being.

Avidyā (lit., *nescience*) When pure Consciousness associates itself with any object, the limited identification that results from such an association is the technical meaning of spiritual ignorance. In Shaivism, the ignorance is not indeterminate but a self-imposed condition resulting from the exercise of the Lord's power of absolute freedom.

Bhakti (lit., *devotion*) Natural devotion for God, Guru, or the pure Self that arises gradually as a result of meditation practice.

Bhakti mārga (lit., *path of devotion*) Yogic practice where the focus of attention is on cultivating devotional feelings and surrender to God as a way of purifying the ego.

Bhāva The inner feeling a yogin cultivates when practicing meditation or any other yogic discipline.

Bīja (lit., *seed*) The seed syllables that correspond to the primary energies behind the creation, sustenance, and dissolution of the universe. Some mantras are combinations of seed syllables. *Bīja* syllables are sometimes inserted between the words that make up a mantra in order to endow them with greater potency. *Bīja* can also signify the mental impressions that are part of the veiling mechanism that helps maintain individuality. See *saṃskāras*.

Brahmacharya Total control of the mind and sense organs, especially of the sexual impulse. *Brahmacharya* means sexual continence, specifically the preservation of one's vital energies.

Brahman The primary name used to point to the eternal, changeless Awareness. Brahman is found within the Upanishadic tradition. To that extent it is the same as the Anuttara or Paramashiva of the Shaivite tradition.

Brahmarandhra The energy plexus located at the crown of the head. Meditators draw down Shakti through the *brahmarandhra*. Conversly, Shakti also can escape the body through the same center.

Buddhi (lit., *intellect*) The innate intelligence aspect of the mind which is commonly obscured by the other veiling aspects of the mind (ego and thought) that, when made spotless through meditation, is able to reflect the pure Consciousness that is its source.

Chakra (lit., *wheel*) The system of major and minor energy plexuses found throughout the subtle body that govern different aspects of the body and mind. Through meditation, the chakras and connecting energy channels are purified in preparation for the lightning ascent of the Kundalini Shakti.

Chin mudrā A seal made with the hands whereby the thumb touches the forefinger, forming a circle. The hands are placed palms down just above the knees. For a similar hand gesture, see *jñāna mudrā*, where the hands are placed palms up.

Chit Kundalini One of three manifestations of Kundalini that yogins experience when they penetrate the center of any two points, such as the point between the breaths or the point between two thoughts. When *Chit* Kundalini manifests, it rises through all the chakras in a single flash, and not progressively as in *Prāna* Kundalini. *Chit* Kundalini only manifests in a yogin who is entirely devoid of worldly desires.

Chit purusha The limited individual subjective consciousness that results from the operation of the power of *māyā*. Due to the functioning of *māyā* the individual soul is subjected to limitations of action, knowledge, time, attachment, and natural law.

Darshan (lit., *sight*) Coming face to face or experiencing the presence of God, Guru, or a consecrated idol. *Darshan* can also be internal, meaning the inner-witnessing of one's own Self.

Dhāraṇā The effort to concentrate on a single object of perception. *Dhāraṇā* also means guided visualizations or guided meditations.

Dharma-megha samādhi The final *samādhi* discussed in Patañjali's *Yoga Sūtra*, here equated with permanent Self-awareness that continues unabated regardless of whether the yogin is awake, dreaming, or in deep sleep.

Dhyāna (lit., *meditation*) The attempt to make our mind rest in its own innate awareness by turning our attention in on itself.

Dīkshā (lit., *initiation*) Initiation is a technical term that means a transmission of Shakti from Guru to disciple that activates or awakens the Kundalini Shakti.

Gunas (lit., *qualities*) Three principles that emanate from *prakṛti tattva* (*sattva*, *rajas*, and *tamas*) of harmony and light, activity and passion, and dullness and ignorance, respectively. Within a yogic context, the *gunas* affect the mind, making practice easy or difficult.

Guru mānasa pūjā Mental worship of the Guru. Any visualized sequence of worship of the Guru's person; this can include the waving of lights or the offering of flowers, fruits, and other pure objects.

Guru tattva The Guru principle. A term used to denote the liberating power of the Lord's grace which is ever flowing. The physical Guru is understood to be a personification of the power of grace, whose primary function is to liberate the soul from individualized awareness.

Iḍā Nāḍi One of the primary subtle energy channels that runs the length of the spine on the left side of the central channel. The *iḍā nāḍī* is considered lunar or cool and governs the functioning of the mind.

Ishwar A name for God or the governing aspect of pure Awareness that controls the workings of creation.

Jalandhara bandha An important lock in which the chin is pressed down onto the suprasternal notch at the base of the throat. The yogic locks, such as *mūla*, *uḍḍiyāna*, and *jalandhara bandha*, which occur naturally in meditation, have the purpose of arresting or manipulating the flow of energy through the subtle system of energy channels, with the aim of preparing the body for the ascent of the Kundalini Shakti.

Japa The silent repetition of a mantra.

Jñāna mārga (lit., *path of knowledge*) Yogic practice where the focus of attention is on cultivating a deep intellectual understanding of yogic philosophy, which enables the practitioner to successfully locate and identify with their I-feeling.

Jñāna mudrā (lit., *seal of knowledge*) A seal made with the hands whereby the thumb touches the forefinger, forming a circle. The hands are placed palms up just above the knees. Compare with *chin mudrā*.

Jñānin A term commonly found within the Vedantic tradition used to denote a fully enlightened being.

Kashmir Shaivism An umbrella terms used to denote the synthesis of four major Tantric schools (*Pratyabhijñā*, *Kula*, *Krama*, and *Spanda*) which are all based on the authority of a body of scripture known as the *Āgamas*. The synthesis of the four schools was brought about by the great tenth-century Master, Sri Abhinavagupta. See Anuttara Trika.

Kevala nirvikalpa samādhi A term used by Sri Ramana Maharshi to denote a temporary state of closed-eyed meditative absorption that ends once the meditator rises from his or her seat. In this state the ego is subdued but not destroyed.

Krama mudrā (lit., *gesture of sequence*) An automatic process that unfolds at the very edge of final enlightenment where the eyes open and close so that the meditator feels that the objective, external world is being absorbed into and becoming part of his subjective I-consciousness. The process of *krama mudrā* can completely unfold in a single meditation session or it can take hundreds of sessions to reach its end point.

Kriyā (lit., *action*) Subtle processes initiated by the accumulation of Shakti in a meditator whereby the spiritual energy works at all levels (physical, mental, subtle, and causal) to remove illnesses, clear energy blockages, and expunge old mental impressions in preparation for the ascent of the Kundalini Shakti.

Kumbhaka Breath retention that occurs spontaneously under the will of the Shakti; it is designed to hasten the union of the incoming and outgoing breaths leading to *samādhi*.

Kundalini (lit., *coiled one*) Kundalini is Consciousness manifested as dynamic energy, the residual energy of creation that is found in all living beings which is responsible for keeping the individual in bondage or, when awakened, for elevating him or her to a state of Self-awareness.

Kundalini Shakti Once the Kundalini is awakened through the process of *shaktipāt*, her workings and presence in the body and mind in the form of subtle energy is referred to as Kundalini Shakti.

Lambika Four subtle passages located on the soft palate near the pit of the throat. Two are closed and two are open. Just prior to the ascent of the Kundalini Shakti, the left *lambikā* closes and the right one opens, allowing the collected breath to be sipped down into the central channel.

Laya (lit., *abeyance, dissolution*) A temporary state of submergence or abeyance where the ego and the mind seem to completely disappear into pure Consciousness, only to emerge again as soon as the meditator ends his or her session.

Mādhyama (lit., *middle*) The center point between two objects or movements.

Mahāvākyas (lit., *great sayings*) Four great statements on the nature of the Self found in each of the Vedas. Here the term *mahāvākya* is applied more broadly to include any statement a yogin repeats to himself to affirm his identity with the absolute Self.

Mahāvikāsha (lit., *great expansion*) The process whereby the direct cognition of the pure Self is extended outward to encompass the entire objective sphere.

Mala (lit., *impurity*) Three innate contractions of Consciousness that envelop and bind the individual soul. The three *malas* are: *āṇava*, *māyīya*, and *kārma*. *Āṇava mala* is the atomic or root impurity that creates a sense of incompleteness. *Māyīya mala* creates the experience of endless diversity, and *kārma mala* creates the experience of limited action and authorship.

Manas (lit., *mind*) Denotes the thinking and selecting aspect of the mind which filters the information presented to the intellect.

Māyā (lit., *illusion*) An obscuring and veiling power of God which gives rise to the five limitations that bind the soul: action, knowledge, time, attachment, and natural law. Māyā is sometimes referred to as "ignorance" and "illusion" in the Vedantic tradition but in Shaivism is considered an expression of the Lord's absolute power of freedom.

Mudrā (lit., *gesture*) Physical gestures, usually of the hands (but may also be of the eyes and tongue), that occur spontaneously under the inspiration of the accumulated Shakti. *Mudrās* arise in order to assist the Shakti to clear blockages in the body and subtle energy channels.

Mūla bandha An important lock in which the perineal area or cervical area is pulled in and upward. The yogic locks, which occur naturally in meditation, have the purpose of arresting or manipulating the flow of energy through the subtle system of energy channels with the aim of preparing the body for the ascent of the Kundalini Shakti.

Mūlādhāra chakra The lowest of the seven major chakras located along the spine. *Mūlādhāra* is located at a point near the perineum region.

Nāda (lit., *sound*) The inner, unstruck sounds that manifest at a certain stage in meditation. *Nāda* is highly purifying and indicates that the yogin is nearing the deeper levels of *samādhi*.

Nāḍi (lit., *channel*) A extensive network of subtle energy channels that resemble the nervous system. Life energy flows through these channels, which intersect within the seven major chakras. The *nāḍis* are said to be 72,000 in number. Three are of primary importance: the *iḍā*, *piṅgala*, and *sushumṇā*.

Neti, neti (lit., *not this, not this*) An intellectual method at arriving at the understanding that the essence and continuity of a human being is based on Consciousness, and not the body or the mind. The practice involves grasping the fact that cognition of an object of perception implies a division between the perceiver and the perceived, meaning that we cannot be the object of perception. The practice also involves understanding that objects of perception are inherently unstable, since they are transient by nature, in contrast to our continuous and unchanging sense of being.

Nidrā (lit., *sleep*) *Nidrā* does not refer to ordinary sleep, but to the elevated state of awareness a yogin attains after penetrating the point between waking and dreaming or dreaming and deep sleep. *Nidrā* is usually attained in formal meditation when the mind becomes one-pointed enough and the body pure enough to break through the sleep barrier. True entrance into *nidrā* is a dramatic event and a major milestone in the life of a meditator.

Nimīlana samādhi (lit., *closed-eyed absorption*) The Shaivite umbrella term used to describe closed-eyed meditative absorption where the mind is perfectly quiescent and rests in its source of pure Consciousness.

Nirbīja samādhi In *nirbīja samādhi* the yogin attains full unity awareness, transcending even the limited I-sense. In *nirbīja samādhi* all latent impressions have been expunged. It is the final level of closed-eyed *samādhi* that precedes the attainment of the final opened-eyed unity awareness.

Nirvicāra samādhi In *nirvicāra samādhi* the yogin is completely merged with subtle objects of perception such as the root powers of seeing, hearing, tasting, etc. At this level of absorption, there is no ideation regarding the object of perception being concentrated upon.

Nirvikalpa samādhi In *nirvikalpa samādhi* there is full meditative absorption devoid of any ideation or latent impressions. It is the Advaita Vedanta term for final closed-eyed *samādhi* which can be equated with the *nirbīja* level of *samādhi* found in Patañjali's classification.

Nirvitarka samādhi In *nirvitarka samādhi* the mind, which has been concentrating deeply on an object of focus, fuses into the object through the elimination of any thought association of the object in question. In other words, the sounds, letters, thoughts, and memory that are associated with the object disappear from the meditator's mind, allowing direct and unmediated knowledge and identification with the object of perception.

Nyāsa (lit., *placing*) In *nyāsa* the meditator takes a sacred image (of a Guru, deity, point of light, diagram, and so on) and mentally places it in different parts of the body. Usually the image is placed along the seven chakras. *Nyāsa* is a form of worship whose purpose is to purify and bless the body of the yogin through the installation of an image that is vibrant with spiritual power.

Ojas (lit., *vitality*) *Ojas* is the spiritual vitality that a yogin develops as a result of the accumulation of Shakti through meditation and in particular through the preservation of sexual fluid. In this sense, *ojas* is simply the storehouse of Shakti that is distributed throughout the body. However, Swami Muktananda taught that *ojas* is an actual yellow fluid that accumulates in the bone marrow. Proper accumulation of *ojas* is absolutely necessary to be able to withstand the intense heat and forces generated by higher levels of meditative absorption. Likewise, entry into *tandrā* is only possible for a yogin who has accumulated a certain amount of *ojas*. The numinous glow seen around yogis or the glow emanating from their skin evidences the presence of *ojas*.

Paramārthasāra (lit., *the essence of the supreme truth*) An important text by Abhinavagupta that discusses the essence of his Trika philosophy in 105 verses.

Pingala nāḍi One of the primary subtle energy channels that runs the length of the spine on the right side of the central channel. The *pingala* is considered solar or hot and governs the functioning of the externalized aspect of awareness.

Prajñā (lit., *consciousness, intelligence*) A Sanskrit word that denotes individual consciousness, awareness, or intelligence.

Prāna The vital energy that courses through the body and sustains life. *Prāna* is derived from the sun, food, and air. It is carried through the breath and is a grosser form of the underlying spiritual Shakti. *Prāna* is commonly referred to as life energy.

Prāna Kundalini One of three manifestations of Kundalini (*Parā, Chit, Prāna*) that yogins experience when they penetrate the center of any two points, such as the point between the breaths or the point between two thoughts. When *Prāna* Kundalini manifests, it rises progressively through each chakra, penetrating the chakra and making it whirl in a clockwise direction, until it rises to the next chakra, repeating the process. *Prāna* Kundalini is located within the human breath.

Pranava The primordial vibration. One of the first stirrings of Consciousness in its movement toward creation articulated through audible sound as "om" or "aum."

Prāṇāyāma The yogic practice of manipulating the breath with the aim to purify the subtle energy channels, still the mind, and awaken the dormant Kundalini Shakti.

Pratyabhijñāhṛdayam (lit., *the heart of the doctrine of recognition*) A key Shaivite text by the eleventh-century Master Kshemaraja that espouses the doctrine of Self-recognition. The text explains that the universe appears as a self-contained reflection within pure Consciousness, and that the universe is not materially different from Consciousness. The *Pratyabhijñāhṛdayam* sets out various means for the individual to recognize or recapture its identity as the pure Self.

Retas (lit., *semen*) The male sexual fluid.

Sabīja (lit., *with seed*) In the *Yoga Sūtra*, *sabīja* refers to meditative states of absorption that still contain the subtle and subconscious latent mental impressions also known as *saṃskāras*.

Sādhaka (lit., *skillful, achiever*) A term broadly used to denote a spiritual aspirant.

Sādhanā Any particular path, method, or practice whose aim is the attainment of Self-awareness.

Sahaja nirvikalpa samādhi Sri Ramana Maharshi's final level of *samādhi* that is continuous and unbroken and persists throughout all three states of waking, dream, and deep sleep.

Sahaja samādhi The final state of continuous opened-eyed *samādhi* where identification with pure Consciousness is continuous and irrevocable. This is enlightenment in the highest sense of the word, where the universe is directly experienced as being non-different from one's own Self.

Sahasrāra chakra (lit., *thousand-spoked center*) The seventh energy plexus located above the crown of the head. Final absorption into Self-awareness can only occur if the Kundalini Shakti is able to reach into the *sahasrāra* chakra.

Samāna One of the five principal functions of *prāna* in the body which is responsible for the equal distribution of energy and nourishment to the entire body.

Samāpatti (lit., *correct acquisition*) Another word for *samādhi*, or meditative absorption.

Samāvesha (lit., *absorption, penetration*) Another word for *samādhi*, or meditative absorption.

Samprajñāta samādhi The initial levels of meditative absorption where the mind is united to an object of contemplation and still filled with latent mental impressions that serve to veil the intellect from the direct awareness of pure Consciousness. Progress through the levels of *samprājñāta samādhi* is marked by the mind's ability to concentrate on increasingly subtle objects of perception, culminating in a direct union with one's I-feeling. Patañjali teaches that one must move gradually from gross to subtle objects of attention, while Sri Ramana Maharshi teaches that one should, if capable, make the subtle I-feeling one's target of attention right from the onset of yogic practice.

Samsāra The repeated cycle of birth and death caused by the momentum of karma that pulls the soul back into embodied existence.

Saṃskāra The large storehouse of mental impressions that are part of the veiling mechanism that helps maintain individuality. When actions are performed or the mind engages in thoughts and emotions, residual traces of the actions and experiences remain within the psychic apparatus. These latent impressions are the cause of an individual's repeated desires, habits, tendencies, and perspectives, and they are responsible for the expression of the personality. The innate *saṃskāras,*which usually promote attachment and aversion, anchor the soul to repeated cycles of birth and death.

Sānanda samādhi In *sānanda samādhi* the mind moves beyond absorption in gross or subtle objects of perception, moving directly into a plane of bliss. Entry into *sānanda samādhi* means the yogin has transcended the plane of the intellect and is residing at the level of the causal body which is experienced as bliss.

Saṅkalpa (lit., *will, intention*) An act of will, a strong intention.

Saṅkalpa dīkshā (lit., *initiation through an act of will*) In terms of initiation, perfected beings can awaken a disciple's Kundalini Shakti without being physically present before the disciple. Even saints who are no longer living can initiate worthy disciples through *saṅkalpa dīkṣā* by appearing in a dream, meditation, or other mystical encounter.

Sasmita samādhi In *sasmita samādhi* the mind becomes absorbed in its own innate I-feeling. This is the most subtle object of perception that the mind can focus on. In reality, since there is not one Self searching for another Self, absorption into the I-sense means that pure Awareness is focusing on itself while still tainted by a veil of ego and latent impressions. Here the I-sense is still the limited sense of individuality that rises like a phantom between the pure Self and the body-mind. In *sasmita samādhi* we can state that the ego itself becomes the object of perception.

Satchidānanda A compound word meaning "being, consciousness, and bliss." It is the Vedantic term used to describe the qualities or properties of the pure Self.

Sati (*Pāli*: lit., *mindfulness*) See *vipassanā*.

Satsang A gathering of spiritual seekers with the purpose to discuss yogic philosophy or engage in yogic practices.

Savicāra samādhi In *savicāra samādhi* the meditator becomes absorbed in subtle objects of perception that include the instruments of cognition or the subtle aspects of the five senses.

Savikalpa samādhi In *savikalpa samādhi* the yogin attains meditative absorption with the support of ideation. It is the Advaita Vedanta term for the initial levels of closed-eyed *samādhi* which can be equated with all the levels of *samprājñāta samādhi* found in Patañjali's classification.

Savitarka samādhi The first level of *samādhi* in Patañjali's classification where the mind is completely fused to a gross object of focus such as a mantra, image of the Guru, and so forth. Although the mind is fused to the object, causing the perceiver or cognizer to seemingly disappear, there is still thought-based knowledge of the object present in the mind.

Shaivism A dominant school or sect within Hinduism that reveres Lord Shiva as the ground of all existence. Shaivism is practiced in all corners of India. There are philosophical distinctions among the various schools of Shaivism, some espousing dualist metaphysics, while others argue in favor of non-dual metaphysics. The words "dual" and "non-dual" refer to the degree of separation, if any, between the underlying pure Consciousness and objective creation.

Shakti (lit., *power*) The primordial and dynamic power that manifests as the universe. Shakti is also the spiritual energy that enables the contracted, individualized consciousness to regain its state of pure subjectivity. All processes in yoga are enabled and guided by the workings of Shakti. *Prāna* and Kundalini are two types of Shakti that are present in human beings. Shakti is not an inanimate force, but the supremely intelligent and free power of Awareness.

Shaktipāt (lit., *descent of power, descent of grace*) An initiatory event in which the spiritual aspirant is filled with Lord Shiva's liberating power, usually through the agency of a Guru, causing the root impurity or *ānava mala* to be destroyed. *Shaktipāt* can be experienced in nine levels of strength depending on the recipient's capacity to withstand it. *Shaktipāt* is also equated with the connection to the Guru's Shakti that awakens the dormant Kundalini.

Shiva Sūtras Seventy-seven aphorisms on the supreme unity of Consciousness and the individual that are accepted as revealed directly by Lord Shiva. The *Shiva Sūtras* is a key Sanskrit text of what is today known as Kashmir Shaivism which asserts the non-dual nature of Consciousness and the means to attain Self-awareness.

Siddha (lit., *accomplished*) An accomplished yogin who has reached a level of attainment where they are able to transmit Shakti in order to awaken the Kundalini Shakti of other aspirants. Siddha is commonly used to denote a fully liberated being, although the term can also indicate a yogin who possesses supranormal yogic powers but who has not yet attained final Self-awareness or *sahaja samādhi*.

Sukhāsana (lit., *easy pose*) A hatha yoga sitting posture where the spine is erect and the legs are comfortably crossed.

Sushumnā nāḍī The principal subtle energy channel that runs from the base of the spine, terminating at the crown of the head. The six other energy plexuses rest along the *sushumnā*. When after prolonged practice, the incoming and outgoing breaths are harmonized, they collect at the back of the throat and are sipped down into the central channel, leading to the true rise of the Kundalini Shakti and the higher levels of *samādhi*.

Svādhishthāna chakra The sacral chakra located along the spine near the coccyx. Among its many qualities, *svādhishthāna* governs the rise and fall of sexual energy.

Svātantrya Shakti The absolute independent freedom of Lord Shiva. The power of the Lord to do as he wishes, usually in reference to the impulse to create, maintain, and dissolve creation throughout unending cycles of time.

Tamas (lit., *darkness*) Dull, grounding energy. One of the three *gunas* that emerge from *prakṛti tattva*.

Tandrā A higher state of consciousness that lies within the juncture between waking and dreaming or dreaming and deep sleep. Yogins who have sufficiently purified their bodies, minds, and vital energy through deep meditation are able to pass into the state of *tandrā*, which is highly sensorial in nature. Passage through *tandrā* purifies and eliminates many of the embedded latent impressions that veil the mind, preparing the yogin for entry into the higher states of *samādhi*. The concept of *tandrā* is sometimes referred to as *nidrā* or *turīya*.

Tanmātras (lit., *subtle elements*) The *tanmātras* are the subtle powers of the five senses (smell, hearing, touch, sight, and taste) that correspond to the five types of matter (earth, air, water, fire, and ether) respectively. Accordingly, from the element of earth rises the *tanmātra* of smell. It is not smell, per se, but the subtle power behind the act of smelling. When yogins reach the level of *savicāra samādhi* they are able to take any of the five *tanmātras* as their object of concentration.

Tantrāloka (lit., *light of the tantras*) Abhinavagupta's magnum opus which presents a detailed analysis of his Anuttara Trika synthesis of numerous tantric paths.

Tantric tradition An umbrella term that includes Tantric scriptures, yogic practices, and rituals designed to elevate a human being from experiencing him or herself as an individual to the direct non-dual awareness that he or she and the entire universe are nothing but pure Consciousness. Another distinct feature of tantra is its overt focus on the Kundalini Shakti as the guiding and enabling power that makes it possible for consciousness to unfold.

Tapas See *tapasyā*.

Tapasyā (lit., *heat, asceticism*) *Tapasyā* operates at several levels. At the most basic level, it means self-control, i.e., restraining desires that lead us toward identification with the body-mind. At a deeper level, the friction between the breath and the mantra causes the mind to grow one-pointed, and the latter causes Shakti to accumulate in the body, filling it with "yogic fire." As the mind becomes stronger in its ability to focus, the storehouse of old mental impressions begin to rise to the surface to be expunged, and this is also another form of "yogic fire." At the highest level, *tapasyā* means that our attention is fully absorbed in our I-consciousness.

Tattvas (lit., *principle*) A classification system that sets out thirty-six principles of creation from Shiva, the primordial Consciousness, down to a blade of grass. *Tattvas* are the different phases of Consciousness as it involutes and contracts from its formless, expanded state down to the five gross elements.

Tejas (lit., *light*) Here the term does not refer to material light but to the vitality that accumulates in the body when the Shakti that is brought down in meditation is not wasted. Specifically, the practice of celibacy is what retains *tejas* in the body, which later converts into *ojas*.

Turīya (lit., *the fourth*) The final state of Consciousness that is devoid of the tripartite division between knower, knowledge, and object known. *Turīya* is another word for pure subjectivity, the domain of pure Awareness which contains all of creation. The term *turīya* is sometimes used to refer to the lower, highly visual state of Consciousness that is found when the yogin penetrates the juncture between waking and dreaming or dreaming and deep sleep. See *tandrā*.

Udāna One of the five vital energies responsible for the ascent of the Kundalini Shakti after the *prāna* and *apāna* are equalized and sipped down into the central channel.

Uḍḍiyāna bandha An important lock in which the abdominal muscles are drawn in and upward. The yogic locks, which occur naturally in meditation, have the purpose of arresting or manipulating the flow of energy through the subtle system of energy channels with the aim of preparing the body for the ascent of the Kundalini Shakti.

Unmilana samādhi (lit., *opened-eyed absorption*) The Shaivite umbrella term used to describe opened-eyed meditative absorption where the mind is perfectly quiescent and rests in its source of pure Consciousness despite the yogin moving about in the waking state. See *sahaja samādhi*.

Vajrāsana (lit., *diamond pose*) A hatha yoga posture where the meditator folds his legs beneath him or her and sits over the heels in a kneeling posture.

Vāsanā (lit., *tendencies, inclinations*) A term used to denote the storehouse of mental impressions and tendencies that drive desires and rise as thoughts. See *saṃskāra*.

Vedantic tradition Refers to the yogic tradition of Vedanta which embodies the metaphysics of the scriptures known as the *Upanishads*. Vedanta also refers to the combined teachings of the *Upanishads*, the *Brāhma Sūtras*, and the *Bhagavad Gīta*. Like Shaivism, within Vedanta there are distinct philosophical schools, some espousing dualist metaphysics, while others argue in favor of non-dual metaphysics. See Advaita Vedanta.

Vidyut (lit., *electricity*) Here the term does not refer to material electricity but to the vitality that accumulates in the body when the Shakti that is brought down in meditation is not wasted. Specifically, the practice of celibacy is what retains the *vidyut* in the body, which later converts into *ojas*.

Vijñāna Bhairava A key Tantric text within the tradition of Kashmir Shaivism that sets out 112 centering techniques to gain immediate access to supreme Self-awareness. Although the text makes it look as if anyone can practice the exercises or contemplations presented throughout, in reality the *Vijñāna Bhairava* is a manual for highly advanced practitioners whom have already attained a high degree of closed-eyed *samādhi*.

Vipassanā (Pāli: lit., *right knowledge, insight*) A popular Buddhist meditation method where all cognitions and perceptions are to be viewed in a passive and detached way in order to enhance the knowledge that all phenomena are transient and impermanent. *Vipassanā* also cultivates the conscious separation between observer and observed, *sati* (mindfulness), which is the first step in allowing the I-consciousness to become aware of itself. However, *vipassanā* is criticized for not explicitly teaching how to turn one's attention inward, which is a necessary condition for enlightenment to unfold.

Vīryā (lit., *strength, virility*) Another step in the production of *ojas*. When Shakti is brought down in meditation, it accumulates in the body as long as it is not wasted. Specifically, the practice of celibacy is what retains the *vīryā* in the body, which later converts into *ojas*.

Vyāna One of the five principal functions of *prāna* in the body which pervades the entire body.

Yantra A spiritual or mystical diagram employing geometric shapes and colors that illustrates a particular manifestation of consciousness. Yantras can depict the chakras, sacred syllables, the microcosm of the human body, or the macrocosm of the *tattvas*. Yantras are used as meditative objects of focus that help develop concentration and purification of mind.

Yoga Sūtra An ancient text ascribed to Patañjali that discusses in minute detail the nuances relating to the phases of meditative absorption, yogic practice, the supranormal powers obtained through concentration, and the characteristics of liberation. Philosophically, The *Yoga Sutra* does not belong to either the Kashmir Shaivism or Advaita Vedanta traditions but is located within the Samkhya tradition. That said, the text is studied and revered by all traditions and is considered the most important and fundamental text on the practice of meditation.

ABOUT THE AUTHOR

Andres Pelenur has been meditating and studying yogic scriptures for over twenty years. He is a disciple of the great saint Bhagawan Nityananda of Ganeshpuri (1897–1961), having been initiated directly by Bhagawan in what is termed *sankalpa dīkshā* (initiation through the will of a Guru). Andres received mantra *dīkshā* (initiation into mantra) from Gurumayi Chidvilasananda and received training in multiple yogic disciplines at her ashram in South Fallsburg, New York. He has traveled extensively throughout India, meditating in numerous ashrams including Bhagawan's ashram in Kanhangad, Kerala, and in Ganeshpuri, Maharashtra. Andres holds a BA in English from McGill University and a JD from the University of Toronto, Faculty of Law.

INDEX

Dyczkowski, Mark S.G.
  The Doctrine of Vibration, 16

ego
  and body-mind, 57–58
  collapsed via stillness of mind,
    58
  I-consciousness as, 39–40, 92
  influence on consciousness,
    6–7
  mind as eliminating, 61–63
  neutralizing/purifying, 6–7, 19
  Ramakrishna on, 158
  and *saṃskāras*, 137
  and thoughts, 64
exercise, 167

fire of yoga (*tapas*), 107–11
first principles, 5–20
  greatest obstacle facing
    spiritual seekers, 7–10
  observations about Vedanta
    and Kashmir Shaivism,
    13–20
  pure Consciousness/
    Awareness, 5–6
  scriptural traditions, 10–13
free will, 32–33

garima, 125n
God
  grace of, 44
  Ishwar, 190
  meditating on, 54–55
  powers of, 25, 27
  will of, 32–33
Godman, David, xv
grace vs. self-effort, 30–33
grogginess, 119
Gunaratana, Bhante, 51
gunas (qualities), 6n5, 71, 138, 176,
  189, 202
Guru mānasa pūjā (mental worship
  of the Guru), 190
Gurus, 21–35

authentic/true, 21, 29, 105
connection to, 24–25
as embodying pure
  Consciousness, 28
evaluating teachers, 29–30
false gurus, 25–28, 104–5
grace of, 19, 23, 25, 30–34
immature seekers vs. mature
  devotees of, 22
initiation of disciples, 22–23,
  26–29
as inner Self, 23–24, 31
living, 29–30
nature of, 24–29
need for, 105n
nyāsa (placing the Guru in the
  body), 79–81
physical, as proof of
  enlightenment, 23–24
and self-effort vs. grace, 30–33
Self-realization without
  physical presence of, 21–23,
  25–27
on sexual activity vs. celibacy,
  152–53
without physical presence of
  Gurus, 21–23, 25–27
worship of, 79, 190
vs. yogins, 21–22
See also individual Gurus
Guru tattva (Guru principle), 25,
  190

hāṃsa (mythical swan), 17n
heart chakra, 76, 88–89, 95
Hindu monasteries, 145, 156
humility, 32

I-consciousness/-feeling, 37–55
  and being unconscious, 38–39
  as ego, 39–40, 92
  focusing attention on, 64, 176
  as the ground of our existence,
    37–39
  the mind's four aspects, 40–41

Index

vs. objects of experience, 38, 51
and pure Awareness, 9–10
Sadhu Om on traditional
   practices, 45–50
Sadhu Om's teachings,
   qualifying, 50–55
self-awareness by shifting
   attention to, 40–45
and suppressing thoughts,
   43–44
iḍā nāḍī, 108, 190
India as a holy land, 10
inner renunciation, 171
intellect
   as an aspect of mind, 40–41, 57
   buddhi, 40, 188
   identified with body-mind,
     58, 111
   purification of, 58–60
Ishwar (a name for God), 190
isitvam, 125n

jalandhara bandha (a yogic lock),
   100, 118, 118n, 121, 190
James, Michael, xv, 17
Janananda, Swami, 23
japa (mantra repetition), 46, 48–
   53, 93, 190
jñāna-mārga (Vedantic path of
   knowledge), 104, 190
jñāna mudrā (seal of knowledge),
   77, 190–91
jñānins (Self-aware beings), 27,
   66, 191

kārma mala, 6n5, 59
Kashmir Shaivism, vii
   as all-embracing, 13, 15
   defined, 191
   Masters, 16
   names of *samādhi* in, 141–42
   on open- vs. closed-eyed
     samādhi, 139
   popularity, 15
   on sexual desire, 146–47

vs. Vedanta, 13, 16–17
   See also Anuttara Trika
Kaula Shaivism, 139
krama mudrā, 92, 125–26, 141, 191
kriyās (spontaneous movements
   during meditation), 95, 99–
   106, 114, 116–19, 127–28, 191
Kshemaraja, 24–25, 197
kumbhaka, 118–19, 119n77, 191
Kundalini (coiled one), 192
Kundalini Shakti (dynamic power
   of Consciousness)
   awakening of, 22
   control of vs. surrender to, 1
   defined, 192
   rise of, 22, 91–92, 126–27, 141,
     149
   surrender to, 19
   of true Gurus, 21

laghima, 125n
Lakshmanjoo, Swami
   on *Chit* Kundalini, 127
   influence/stature, xvi, 2, 12–13
   on the *lambikā*, 124
   lifestyle of, 172
   on meditating with
     continually refreshed
     awareness, 92
   Ramana's influence on, 13
   on *tandrā*, 120, 123
   on *tanmātras*, 121
   on *turīya*, 119n78, 120–21, 123
   on visions, 123–24
   as a voice of wisdom, xvi
lambikā (passages on the soft
   palate), 124, 192
Law of Attraction, 45n
laya (abeyance), 50, 192
liberation
   from bondage, 6–7
   dharma-megha samādhi as,
     138–39
   via thought, 62–63
   who attains liberation, 57–66

Index

resolve/commitment, 70, 75, 115
seat, approaching, 76
seat, taking, 76–77
time, 70–71
woolen *āsana* (seat), 74–76
mind
  ego eliminated by, 61–63
  four aspects of, 40–41, 57
  as not conscious, 57
  See also ego; stillness of mind
mind-body
  Awareness identified with, 42–43, 57–58
  Consciousness as producing, 7–8
  Self identified with, 59–60
monasteries, 145, 156, 175
mudrā (gesture), 193
Muktananda, Swami, 102
mūla bandha, 118, 118n, 193
mūlādhāra chakra, 79, 101, 125, 127, 161, 193
Muruganar, xv, 173

nāda (unstruck sounds), 89, 194
nāḍis (subtle energy channels), 5, 107–9, 114, 128, 148–49, 190, 194, 196
  See also *sushumnā nāḍi*
Natanananda, Swami, 173
navel chakra, 88–89
Neem Karoli Baba, 29
neti, neti ("not this, not this"; negation method), 18, 46–48, 50–51, 194
nicotine, 172
nidrā (sleep), 119, 194
night emissions, 168
nirvikalpa samādhi (closed-eyed, thoughtless, non-dual Awareness), 21, 65–66
Nisargadatta Maharaj
  on change, 172–73
  and Gurus, 23

influence/stature, 19
lifestyle, 172
on seeking light and sound, 104
Self-awareness attained, 23
as a true Guru, 29
niyama (observances), 131n
nyāsa (placing the Guru in the body), 79–81, 195

objects
of experience, 38, 51
first-, second-, and third-person, 38–39
of perception, 49, 54, 132
samādhi via merging into external objects, 49–50
ojas (vitality), 148–49, 159n, 163, 196
Om Guru Om, 53
Om, 93, 95
Om Namaḥ Shivāya, 26, 53, 86–89, 91, 93
Om Namo Nārāyaṇāya, 53
Om Sai Ram, Ram, 53
orgasm, 147, 149, 162, 166
  See also lust

pāda pūjā (adoration of the feet), 79
para (supreme) level, 88n
Paramārthasāra (Abhinavagupta), 58–59
paramārthasāra (essence of supreme truth), 196
paśyantī (casual) level, 88n
Patañjali's *Yoga Sūtra* on samādhi, 131–41, 143
  asamprajñāta samādhi, 137–38, 142, 186
  on beginners' focus on objects of perception, 49
  defined, 206–7
  dhāraṇā, 78n, 131, 131n, 140
  dharma-megha samādhi, 138–39, 141–42, 189

Index

Index

Shaligram, Swami, 29
Shiva (pure Consciousness), 14–16, 25
   See also Consciousness, pure
Shiva Sūtras, 9, 15, 24–25, 32, 37, 83, 144, 201
siddhas (accomplished yogins), 201–2
sleep and sexual desire, 167
smoking, 172
snakebite, symbolism of, 102, 102n70
So'ham, 53, 93–94
sounds, divine inner, 89n
speech levels, 88, 88n
spiritual pride, 104–5
stillness of mind (meditative absorption)
   Consciousness experienced via, 1
   ego collapsed via, 58
   and length of breath, 110
   terms for, 7, 198
   See also *samādhi*
subtle body, 1–2n, 5n
suffering, grace via, 30–31
sukhāsana (a yoga sitting posture), 202
sushumnā nāḍī, 103, 108, 110, 141, 147, 202
svātantrya Shakti (free will of Lord Shiva), 202

tamas (darkness), 6n5, 71, 189, 202
tandrā (a visual state of consciousness)
   after piercing the sleep barrier, 88, 91–93, 119
   celibacy required for, 152
   defined, 202–3
   Lakshmanjoo on, 120, 123
   passage through, 120–24, 127–28
   Patañjali on, 128, 140
   and *sādhanā*, 121–22

time needed to attain, 143
tanmātras (subtle elements), 121, 121n, 140, 203
Tantrāloka (Abhinavagupta), 11
Tantrāloka (light of the tantras), 203
Tantric tradition, xvi, 2
   as all-embracing, 14
   burning everything into sameness, 163
   defined, 51, 203
   Five Jewels, 139, 139n
   Kundalini Shakti as focus of, 104
   Pratyabhijñāhṛdayam, 9, 176, 197
   sexual rites, 146
   synthesis of schools of (*see* Kashmir Shaivism)
   three Ms, 139, 139n
   vs. Vedanta, 51, 104
   See also *Vijñāna Bhairava*
tapasyā/tapas (heat; asceticism), 111, 149, 203–4
tattvas (principles of consciousness), 11, 204
tejas (light), 149, 204
thoughts
   as an aspect of mind, 40–41, 57
   breathing in light, breathing out thoughts, 78–79
   fear of transcending, 66
   as flowing streams of consciousness, 83–84
   liberation via, 62–63
   lust caused by, 165–66
   manas, 40, 193
   racing, 83
   Self/Self-awareness/-realization obscured by, 51, 62
   as sticky and seductive, 64–66
   suppressing, 43–44
three Ms, 139, 139n
transcendental body, 2n
transmigration, 111